Praise for *Mind Ov*

Evan's *Mind Over Money* is one of the be:
and, at heart, most sophisticated books on personal finance that I've read
(and I've read a few).

Alan Kohler, Editor-in-Chief of Eureka Report, finance reporter on *ABC News*,
columnist for *The New Daily* and Adjunct Professor at Victoria University

As an experienced market strategist, I have often relied on Evan's investment
insights, but it's his ability to make us question what really makes us tick that's
the real highlight here. Financial wellbeing and freedom starts with becoming
financially self-aware. Evan does a great job of helping us discover the
best financial versions of ourselves.

Effie Zahos, Editor-at-Large of Canstar, money expert for *The Today Show*,
author of *Ditch the Debt and Get Rich* and *A Real Girl's Guide to Money*,
and independent director of InvestSMART

Normally the only person who benefits from a personal finance book is
the author – but not with this one. Evan teaches you how to fish, rather than
telling you which fish will make you slightly richer right now.

Elysse Morgan, host of ABC's *The Business*, and board member of
Media Super and Hornsby Ku-ring-gai Women's Shelter

Unsurprisingly, Evan has nailed it! Money's not just something we use;
it's attached to our behaviour. When Evan explains why you behave, think
and act in certain ways with money, you better understand that your way
with money is unique to you. Once that penny drops, you will question
your money behaviour for the better. *Mind over Money* is not just a
refreshing, energising read but a must-read for those looking to
understand money and themselves better!

Brooke Corte, host of *Money News*, Nine Radio (3AW, 2GB, 4BC)

MIND OVER MONEY

MIND
OVER
MNEY

Why understanding your money behaviour
will improve your financial freedom

EVAN LUCAS

MAJOR
STREET

For Julia, Harriet and Eloise
My today, tomorrow and beyond all in one

 **MAJOR** First published in 2022 by Major Street Publishing Pty Ltd
STREET info@majorstreet.com.au | +61 421 707 983 | majorstreet.com.au

 A catalogue record for this book is available
from the National Library of Australia

Printed book ISBN: 978-1-922611-48-2
Ebook ISBN: 978-1-922611-49-9

Cover design by Tess McCabe
Internal design by Production Works
Printed in Australia by Griffin Press, an Accredited ISO AS/NZS 14001:2004 Environmental Management System Printer.

Charts provided with kind permission from Refinitiv Datastream.

10 9 8 7 6 5 4 3 2 1

Disclaimer

Contents

Chapter 1	To be human is to be reasonable	1
Chapter 2	You are you, I am me	9
Chapter 3	Money cognition	17
Chapter 4	The five money personalities	35
Chapter 5	When money collides	46
Chapter 6	Liberation: the reality of choice	55
Chapter 7	Time heals all	65
Chapter 8	Money culture	80
Chapter 9	Loving the scary ugly	95
Chapter 10	The elephant paradigm	113
Chapter 11	Control your controllables	121
Chapter 12	Spendvesting	132
Chapter 13	Unreasonable expectations	143

Final thoughts: our minds and money	153
References	159
Glossary	169
About the author	173
Acknowledgements	175
Index	177

Chapter 1

To be human is to be reasonable

To attain any kind of life in this universe of ours appears to be quite an achievement. As humans we are doubly lucky, of course: we enjoy not only the privilege of existence but also the singular ability to appreciate it and even, in a multitude of ways, to make it better.
– Bill Bryson, *A Short History of Nearly Everything*

I vividly remember sitting in a university lecture, wide-eyed and completely overwhelmed by the things I was learning about physical anthropology; you know, Homo erectus, Neanderthal man and of course Homo sapiens – us.

The lecturer unveiled a human skull from a box, looked at us and asked, 'Is this a 10-year-old skull or a 10,000-year-old skull?'

No one responded.

'It's neither,' he continued, 'because it's not a real skull: it's just a mould. But if it was real, you wouldn't be able to tell just by looking at it. We modern humans are basically identical to our Stone Age human ancestors. Our brain size and physique are about the same.'

Think about that: your brain is the same as someone who walked the Earth 35,000 years ago. It hasn't changed in that time.

Scientists, anthropologists and historians largely agree that we were as 'smart' back then as we are now.

Think about the geniuses who have contributed to humanity over centuries and millennia: Socrates, Aristotle, Pythagoras, Hypatia, Galileo, da Vinci, Newton, Einstein, Hawking – the list is long. Then think about the mind power needed to build structures like the Pyramids of Giza, the Roman aqueducts and the Great Wall of China, and the time in history they were built.

The human mind has been able to do a lot of what it does today for thousands and thousands of years. But what is very clearly different today is our lifestyle – our life stresses, our work, our wants, our needs and our desires. Life was relatively straightforward for our ancient relatives: find food and shelter, reproduce and escape peril. Simple. It was a lifestyle of immediate return – find food, eat food; find shelter, sleep; see big hairy beast, run.

The thing about living with immediate returns is that you don't have to think about the concept of time. Time just happens; day becomes night and the seasons flow into each other without being questioned.

In today's fast-moving, never-sleeping world, however, time is a *commodity*. It's something to be mined or put into intervals and sold – think lawyers and their six-minute work units. Time is something we don't have enough of to do what we need (let alone want) to do.

That means making quick decisions, often very complex decisions, almost every waking minute of every day. Research says we make as many as 35,000 decisions daily. And plenty of them involve money.

Think about it. What money decisions did you make before you even started work this morning? You might have considered questions like this:

· Should I pack lunch for work to save money?
· Can I justify paying for a latte on the way to work when I have an espresso machine at home?

2

- Should I pay for my train ticket with cash or card?
- Is the mortgage repayment due today? Do I have enough cash in my account to cover it?

Then you might have gotten even further ahead of yourself:

- Do I need a new job?
- Have I planned for my future?
- Have I planned for my kids' futures?
- Do I need to find more income?
- Do I want to go on a holiday soon?
- Should I think about buying a house?

The list goes on… 35,000 times every day.

It's a mind-boggling array of decisions – and that's before you've even reached midday and started wondering if you should ditch your homemade lunch after all and buy something more appealing from the sushi joint downstairs.

The key point here is that each of these potential questions is a delayed-return decision. The decision you make now has no immediate return; that comes later (or so you hope) – like tomorrow or next week or next year or even next decade, or somewhere even further into the beyond.

This point is core to investing. Can you make a delayed-return decision? Are you able to resist something now to get a greater reward in the future? Can you embrace the concept that time has value, too?

We have to deal with rational and irrational decision-making almost every second of the day. We can all crunch the numbers to make rational decisions. I know if I'm taking a brown-bag lunch to work, I'm probably going to save $10 and spare myself at least 10 minutes queueing at the sushi bar. So, it would be a rational decision to skip the takeaway. But sometimes, that sandwich just seems a bit meh by midday.

All too often we ignore logic and make a choice we know isn't entirely rational. That's because money doesn't just involve finances – it's deeply tied up with our emotions. And emotions are inherently linked to one of the greatest psychological tools humans from ancient times to now possess – choice.

Philosopher Alan Watts said we often experience anxiety about decision-making. We wonder whether we thought the choice through enough, if we considered all the data. The fact is, he says, we can never take enough data into consideration – because data is infinite. Choice, he said, is an 'act of hesitation' before we make a decision. We always doubt whether we're behaving the right way or doing the right thing; we lack confidence. And, he said, 'if you see you lack self-confidence, you will make mistakes through sheer fumbling. If you do have self-confidence, you may get carried away doing the entirely the wrong thing.'

We will talk a lot about choice, decision-making, confidence and doubt in this book: why we have these traits, how they interact and how they are formed. They all affect our interactions with money. What I find so interesting about Watts' view on choice, though, is his suggestion that we make choices that are not necessarily logical but rather irrational, self-deprecating and sometimes against self-interest – yet they are still the 'right' choices. This is where the very analytical, structured, rule-driven world of money clashes with human nature.

Economists like to think they are very rational beings. In the early 1830s political economist John Stuart Mill derived an anthropological being called 'Homo economicus' – the economical man, sometimes also called the 'rational being'. This being has the ability to make infinite rational decisions due to its perfect access to information, its complete self-interest and consistency giving it maximum benefit from its choices.

That description alone should make you realise that the economical man is a robot. Even in this day and age of mass technology, with its algorithms, high-frequency trading, limitless information and artificial intelligence, robots still make the wrong decisions. Why? Because they're programmed by humans. Homo economicus is a unicorn – a mythical being.

Political scientist Herbert A Simon debunked the economical man theory and went on to win a Nobel Prize in economics for his work on bounded rationality. His paper suggested that human beings have a limited capacity to process information, which makes them incapable of being totally rational in their decisions.

We all know from our day-to-day lives that we don't always make rational decisions. Rather than being Homo economicus, we more resemble what German political scientist Timm Beichelt coined 'Homo emotionalis'.

Homo emotionalis has four traits: emotional, social, prone to innate bias and prone to error. Really, it's just another way behavioural-ists like to simplify human nature, but it does invite us to consider broader notions as to why we behave the way we do.

The biases, emotions, social cues and errors that lead to so-called irrational behaviour are learned through experiences. They can be positive for our social functioning but detrimental to rational decision-making. Biases, emotions, social cues and errors are not just an issue for today, but can see us making the same mistakes with money throughout our lives.

The fact is, we are emotional beings, so the way we manage money is driven by our emotions. Think about it: we feel elated when we score a bargain; we feel ripped off if we buy something on the cheap only to find it's priced a few bucks less at another store; and we feel despair when a letter from the tax man that we thought would be a nice refund cheque turns out to be a notice to pay.

Bias, emotion and error are what make us human. Rather than trying to argue that point, maybe we should be celebrating the fact that we are all different, and that's what makes us so unique and wonderful? Our unique humanness explains why our behaviours can be so diverse, even when we're experiencing the same life situation as another person. Money is something we all see differently.

This is something I have always pondered; it is why I wanted to write this book. I have seen highly educated, rational people do the most irrational and human things with money. I've often wondered, how is it that someone making over $300,000 a year can have no money at all? It's most likely because they spend every cent on things they don't need – because they want to keep up certain appearances, or because they have a complete disregard for money and believe it will always be there. Because that's how money has always been to them – available, without a worry it won't be.

This behaviour may seem completely irrational when presented like this, but I have seen examples like this play out time and time again. Because to them it's 'normal'; it's what they have always done with money.

Money is different for everyone. How you use it is unique to you.

What is money to you?

I want to pose a question for you to ponder as you read this book: *what does money mean to you?* The emotional connection we have with money is driven by a wide variety of factors, many of which I'll cover in later chapters. You must identify your unique view on money, because this will influence every financial decision you make. Becoming financially self-aware is key to your financial wellbeing and freedom. No one understands your views on money better than you.

So, are you the kind of person who looks at money with indifference? Is it the stuff of nightmares? Is it just a tool to get you from A to B? Is it something you crave? Or is it something that is attached to your personal identity?

Everyone is different, and everyone behaves in unique ways when it comes to their finances. The main takeaway for now is that emotions have the potential to derail even the best-laid plans. Achieving financial security and freedom means making decisions with your head, not your heart – but this is something we rarely do.

It's important to remember that 'irrational' is not the opposite of 'rational' when it comes to money – far from it. As humans, we are *reasonable*. The reason we react to social cues and form biases, personal characteristics and traits is so that we can navigate life as best we can in a timely and sociably reasonable manner.

And that is a core point to make. As Herbert A Simon said, we are incapable of being totally rational. What is as close to rational as a human can get? Reasonable.

Humans are reasonable because we understand the necessity of trade-offs in decision-making. We can make difficult choices when shock and hardship arises. We know that always making cold, calculated, rational decisions is impossible and will lead us to give up on what we are trying to do.

If we were financially rational all the time, it would probably mean going against the very thing most of us are wanting to achieve: financial choice.

Being reasonable means we can identify when rational decision-making is necessary and when it's not. That is what makes us *us*. We can see when an instant return is the reasonable choice over a delayed return, and vice versa.

The first step in making reasonable financial decisions is to understand the factors that influence your decision-making. Getting your head around this will make your relationship with money and the choices you have that much better.

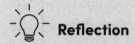 **Reflection**

- When did you last make a *reasonable* money decision, rather than choosing the most *rational* option?
- What does money mean to you?
- Do you consider yourself skilled in delaying gratification?

Chapter 2

You are you, I am me

Be yourself; everyone else is already taken.
– Oscar Wilde

I can't fully explain how I became the person I am today, but I do have a fair idea of the experiences I had over the years that shaped my identity – that made me *me*.

Some of my most formative experiences, particularly to do with money, were shared with my grandfather. Without doubt, he was one of the biggest influences on my behaviour around money. Sometime in the mid-90s I started to realise that my grandfather was rather good at investing. He saw investing not just as a hobby, but as something meaningful that he loved spending time on. I was naturally curious, being a kid, and I started to ask all sorts of questions like, 'Why do you invest?', 'How do you make the right decisions?' and 'What exactly do all those numbers in the middle spread of the newspaper's business section mean?' These conversations with my grandfather nurtured a trait in me that I didn't realise I had until later in life. They helped form me into the *me* of today. They helped shape my identity.

Many of the greatest thinkers of our time have studied identity and how it's formed. English philosopher John Locke was one of the first people to consider the modern concepts of self and identity with his theory of mind. He stated that:

'... a thinking, intelligent being, that has reason and reflection, and can consider itself as itself, the same thinking thing, [can see itself] in different times and places.'

What he is essentially saying is that we have the ability to think about ourselves in the past, present and future in an array of scenarios. This, Locke believed, makes us 'self-conscious beings' who are able to think about ourselves and our learned identity.

If you think about your own life you will be able to identify experiences across the spectrum of time that have helped to form your identity – including your money identity. For example, my time learning about investing with my grandfather is a past experience that has shaped my money identity. I can also identify present and future experiences that are contributing to my money identity: I know that last month my spending was more than I had budgeted for (present experience), and that I am currently saving for my children's education (future experience).

These examples are specific to me, but they fit Locke's idea that I am self-conscious of my learned experiences and how they help form my identity around money both now and into the future.

You will have your own learned experiences that have contributed to your view on money. They are unique to you and have been formed over years of experience, observations, changes and challenges, with cultural beliefs thrown in for good measure.

You can see now why I have named this chapter 'You are you, I am me'. It's a succinct way to say that you use money the way you do, and

I use it another way – and that's to be expected, because we are both human.

Let's make something very clear: no one way of dealing with money is right or wrong. What works for your money identity may not work for others. We will discuss this more in the coming chapters, but for now it's worth keeping in mind that none of this is about judgement or feeling bad about yourself (or others). It's about learning what makes you tick, and working with that to create financial freedom.

Identifying *you*, and the *you* you want to be

Locke helped us understand that our minds are self-conscious: we have the ability to think about ourselves in the past, present and future. The question this raises is one of the biggest in behavioural finance: are *you* today the same *you* you were last week? Or last year? What about 10 or 20 years ago?

To answer this, you need to understand where and when your mind's view on money originated. Only then can you begin to remove old traits and habits that are impeding your current money identity, and replace them with new traits and habits that can lead to financial freedom and therefore more life choices.

Your current money identity developed out of your learned experiences. We are not born with beliefs about money, nor are we born with views on the world, people or politics. Our beliefs are formed as we grow up. Your money beliefs are manifestations of your personal identity which has been formed, moulded and adapted over many years. Think of your money identity like a box, with everything from family and personal experiences, social and cultural norms, relationships and your work life crammed in (see figure 2.1).

Figure 2.1: Influences on your money identity

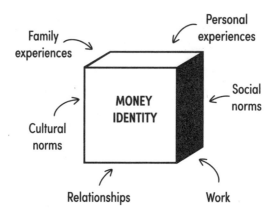

That's the theory – now let's put it into a real-world context by using me as an example.

I am me

I didn't care about money when I was young. I didn't really think about investing in housing, shares or markets until my mid to late 20s, even though my grandfather had exposed me to these ideas. I definitely didn't see myself as a 'money person' like I do today.

Money, to me, was a means to an end. It was to be worked for, saved and then spent on travel. It was that specific to me. Travel was the single most important thing to my identity, and that is how my mind saw money – as a means to express my identity as an adventurer.

My money cycle looked like this:

Make money → Spend on adventures → Repeat

My identity was reinforced each time I completed that cycle:

Travel, adventure and life-defining events = Me

In my mind, my approach to money was fine, because it gave me a way to fit into the wider world. It wasn't a bad way to deal with money, as I was saving before spending and I would never spend more than I had. I never used debt (loans or credit cards) to fund my adventures. But it was limiting, because once my money ran out I had to start again. For me back then, money was for *now*, not the future.

My view on money changed when the world of money collided with my travel and influenced my views – my 'money conscience', if you will. I spent time in Amsterdam, working as an intern at the group headquarters of investment banking company ABN Amro. Investing is all they really talked about. It made me think, 'I need to do that!' I realised by investing I could fund more travel. It wasn't enough to change my money identity then and there, but it was a trigger. I moved from work-save-travel to work-save-invest-travel. So, I still had much the same money identity as before, just with a new habit – investing – added to the mix.

That extra part of my money cycle initially involved investing small amounts. I then added to my investing pool as my mind started to embrace this change. Slowly, over several years, investing became a habit, and that habit became a career that is my money identity today. There was no one experience, no one defining event that moulded my money identity. It was more that each experience tinkered with my consciousness to make a sum total change.

Now, clearly there is more to it than this – these habit changes and decisions were not the only influence on my money identity. Cognitive bias, social and cultural norms, relationships and other life-learned behaviours have also combined to form my money identity and influence my money behaviours.

However, on review, I can see that my current money identity is the result of better money practices coupled with life experiences that have slowly come together to get me to where I am now. I have embraced the identity change I've experienced over the last couple of decades. I now have greater financial choice, because I'm no longer limited by my old money identity of 'make to spend'.

You are you

Now it's your turn. What was your money identity 10 to 20 years ago? Have the habits and traits you had around money back then stayed with you? How have your experiences shaped your money identity since then?

It isn't easy to radically change your core identity. It's concerned with your beliefs, your politics, your perceptions and your biases – and money plays strongly on these. But you will still find that your money identity has matured in the past 10 to 20 years based on the experiences you've had in that time.

For example, if you saw your parents struggle to find a bank willing to lend to them, this will have a lasting impact on how you view the world of money. If you have jumped from credit card to credit card to try to stave off the interest repayments that just keep on building up, your view of saving and debt is likely to be negative. If you invested in markets just before the Global Financial Crisis and saw your investment more than halve in the following seven months, you may not believe that investing will improve your financial wellbeing. Your beliefs and biases will have been deeply affected by these scenarios and, if they were negative experiences, your view on money will most likely have a negative slant.

The experiences of your spouse, siblings, friends and colleagues will also impact your money identity, both positively and negatively, as they are part of the social groups you identify with. Others' habits can and do impact your beliefs more than you might realise. Just as witnessing a parent struggling with money can affect your views, so too can watching your partner fall into the pitfalls of gambling or seeing a friend continue to fall foul to short-term lenders.

The reverse effect can also occur, where others' money habits cause you to view your own money identity and behaviours negatively – as though you are always underwater. Consider that friend or acquaintance who always seems to have more money than you can imagine they make; the person who always seems to be making lavish purchases that you're not sure they can afford. I am certain your thinking goes a little like this: 'How are they doing that? Where do they get that money from? Why can't I do that? Should I be buying a new house or car?'

This is where some of the biggest mistakes with money begin. This kind of thinking leads to one of the worst money-handling behaviours: competing. Competing is fine in sport; even in your work life a little competition can be good for your productivity. But competing with your peers around money leads to risk-taking and, inevitably, mistakes that you may not be prepared for. Your friends' and colleagues' views on money are different from yours. Their financial goals and happiness and your financial goals and happiness will have different measures. We all have different definitions of success.

We'll look at social comparison and competition in more detail later in the book, but for now all you need to remember is this: you are you and I am me. Everyone will behave differently with money because we each have a different money personality.

The next step is to ask yourself: how can I make my money identity align with my financial wants, successes and measures? How can I realign my money identity so that my mind is over money, not under it? That's what we'll explore in this book.

I didn't become good with money overnight, and you shouldn't expect to, either. The change comes from altering your habits and identifying parts of your money identity that need to be redefined – that is, those biases, habits and beliefs (based on social norms and even your culture) that are no longer serving you.

In the next chapter we'll look at one of the biggest things controlling your behaviour and relationship with money: your innate biases.

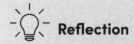 **Reflection**

- What personal experiences contributed to your current view of money?
- What was your money identity 10 to 20 years ago? How has this changed over time?
- Can you identify ways in which your friends and family members' money habits might influence your own?

Chapter 3

Money cognition

Human beings are poor examiners, subject to superstition,
bias, prejudice, and a profound tendency to see what they
want to see rather than what is really there.
– M Scott Peck

Do you understand why you react the way you do to certain situations? Every action you take comes from somewhere. So where is that? If you can understand where your action has come from – why you reacted the way you did – it gives you the power to take steps to improve the behaviours that are not serving you. You'll be the better for it – especially when it comes to money.

In this chapter we'll look at how our minds process the world – how we seamlessly navigate interactions with each other and the material world. When you actually stop and evaluate that statement, I bet you'll find it's something you haven't really thought about. That's because, as a human, you don't have to. I am asking you to evaluate your natural behaviour – the things you do without giving them conscious thought.

Most of us have never stopped to examine the following questions:

· Why do I act in a certain way when I meet someone for the first time?
· Why do I stand behind the last person in the queue at my local cafe, rather than squeezing to the front?
· Why don't I yell out at a cinema or library?
· Why don't I swear or act in a casual manner at a job interview?
· Why do I act a certain way in public?

These may seem like very obvious questions with obvious answers – all fall under the concept of social acceptance. You know that if you were to 'break' the socially acceptable rules – norms – it would create a kind of social chaos.

But how do you differentiate between the right or wrong action in these situations? The answer is: through your learned behavioural biases. These biases are very important to how you function in society and in your day-to-day life. It's not just social interaction that your biases influence; it's also wider choices you make across your entire life. You make these choices without even thinking about them, because they seem 'obvious'.

Think about it. Why do you choose a green pencil over a red pencil? Why do you like one song but not another? Why do you choose a latte over a flat white? Why do you read non-fiction over fiction? You don't really think about these things; you just do them.

The reasoning behind these choices is based on years of experiences, social learning and your formed personality. Once again, you are you.

The human brain is designed to make daily decision-making as easy as possible. Life is complex, so biases – learned behaviours and ideas that we can call on to cut to the chase – are something we embrace readily.

Of course, simplifying decisions leads to errors, as we are effectively cutting corners. Our biases can 'close off' our minds to better options, experiences and longer-term outcomes. They can effectively make us 'mentally blind'. In the world of money and investing this is the opposite of what needs to be done. Money involves structure, repetition and singular long-term resolve.

As we discussed in chapter 2, your relationship with money is heavily influenced by your experiences – how you were brought up, how your parents viewed and dealt with money, who you socialise with, where you work, who you work for or with, and your partner's experiences and views. All these converge to influence and form your money identity. Your money identity then influences your actions. It can lead you to believe a rational decision is an irrational decision, and vice versa. Why? Because your biased view makes it so.

Money biases encompass both cognitive (thought) and emotional biases. While cognitive biases stem from statistical, information-processing or memory errors, emotional biases stem from impulse or intuition, resulting in actions based on feelings instead of facts.

The important thing is to recognise your own biases so you can be aware of how your brain is ticking when you're making decisions. We'll now run through some commonly held behavioural biases that relate to money. Get conscious and be honest here: recognising the biases you hold will help focus your mind when it comes to money.

Loss aversion: losing money hurts more than making it

How many times have you dipped into your wallet for a $50 note that you were sure was there, only to find it missing? What follows is inevitably a search through your clothes, a rummage around the car or even a line-up of your kids against the living room wall as you say, through gritted teeth, 'Now, I know you didn't mean to take it, but hand back the 50 bucks.' The fact is, losing money is emotionally bruising.

Now flip the story. Imagine you reach into the pocket of a pair of jeans and unexpectedly find a $50 note. Your initial reaction is one of joy and even elation, but it's fleeting – it probably doesn't last more than a few minutes. It is not even in the same realm as the emotional experience you felt over the lost $50.

The difference in our emotional barometer between financial loss and gain is real. Behavioural scientists have found we experience far more despair when we lose money compared to when we make a profit. This bias was termed 'loss aversion' by Daniel Kahneman and Amos Tversky in 1979. Loss aversion has the potential to create behaviour that is detrimental to both your financial gains and your losses. It is one of the biggest biases your mind will have to deal with when making money decisions.

Loss aversion has a strong relationship with risk (which we will talk about in detail later in the book): it means we prefer to avoid financial risk, even if the potential returns are better.

Let's take a look at one the tests Kahneman and Tversky used to examine loss aversion in their study. I want you to think about what you would do in this situation – but don't overthink it. Focus on your initial reaction, because that will be your biases acting for you.

If you were given a choice between receiving a guaranteed $900, or having a 90 per cent chance of gaining $1000 but a 10 per cent chance of losing it all, what option would you take?

I would stake you would take the $900. Kahneman and Tversky found the same. Most participants would take the $900 that is presented as 'risk free'. But, when you do the cold, hard maths, the 'risk' is the same. That is:

$$Expected\ value = (\$1000 \times 0.9) + (\$0 \times 0.1) = \$900$$

Now let's reverse the choice. If you had a choice between a guaranteed loss of $900 or a 90 per cent chance of losing $1000 but a 10 per cent chance not losing anything, what option would you take?

I would stake you will take the risk of losing $1000 with the small chance of losing nothing. Again, this is exactly what Kahneman and Tversky found as well.

Like the first scenario, the cold hard maths shows that the expected value is a $900 loss.

It's important to understand that this is your biases influencing you to do what you believe is the right thing. That right thing might not be the 'rational' thing, because rational isn't human. We just need to add our consciousness into the equation to confirm or overrule our bias.

Loss aversion manifests into all sorts of behaviours and, interestingly enough, non-behaviour. If we take the Kahneman and Tversky study into the real world, a 2020 report from the Australian Securities Exchange (ASX) found more than one in three (36 per cent) of Australian adults have never invested. There's a variety of reasons behind this, but the underlying theme is the fear of losing money on the markets.

Whenever I meet a new investor, I start with this question: 'What do you want to get out of investing?'

I should come clean here: I do this to trigger their loss aversion bias. Inevitably they will respond with something to this effect: 'I want my investment to achieve X per cent per annum, *but*' – and there is always a *but* – 'I don't want the capital to decline. How do I do this?'

We will cover the two points raised here in detail later in the book. One is an unreasonable expectation, and the other is explained by the old adage, 'time heals all'.

You can lose value in all investable assets – shares, exchange traded funds (ETFs), bonds, property and even cash. But over time the returns will counter the losses, and there is an almost infinite number of examples that can testify to this. The question is, how much can your mind cope with loss? That comes down to the risk-reward scale.

Ultimately, growing your money is about giving you options, and having options leads to financial freedom. Financial freedom is about having financial choice. Having financial choice allows you to do the things in life you want, while avoiding many of the things you don't want.

So, when it comes to loss aversion you need to think about loss as a relative factor, rather than the be-all and end-all.

I know that is very hard to read. Even the best in the industry still get caught up by loss-making positions in their portfolios or on their bank balances. But what they do better than the rest is to not let the losses impact their long-term view. They keep sight of the goals they are looking to achieve in the future. In other words, they put the loss into perspective, which reduces its emotional impact.

Let's look at an example we all have experience with: retirement savings plans. Most developed nations have a retirement scheme of some description – in Australia it is superannuation; in the US it is the 401(k) scheme. For this example I will concentrate on Australia's superannuation (super).

Super is a fantastic initiative. It's not perfect by any means, but its goal of creating a nation of people who will not have to rely totally on the state during retirement is what makes it one of the best polices of the modern age. It also has the added benefit of creating a whole swathe of people who can achieve financial freedom.

One of the best parts of super is that, by law, your employer must contribute a percentage of your pay packet to your long-term financial wellbeing – which is perfect from a behavioural finance point of view, because it overrides your loss aversion bias. It means that the aversion you have to short-term losses is superseded by the long-term gains investing gives you, because it is mandated.

As we learned in chapter 1, humans still haven't fully evolved to cope with delayed returns – doing something now that might benefit us in the future. Legendary author and behaviouralist James Clear put it perfectly when he said: 'The mismatch between our old brain and our new environment has a significant impact on the amount of chronic stress and anxiety we experience today.'

Loss aversion is one of those major stresses we experience in today's modern world, and it is only compounded by money. We have worked hard for that money so the prospect of losing some of it is hard to take.

This explains why investing, the pinnacle of the delayed-return effect – plays so much with our minds, leading us to defer to our shortcutting bias of loss aversion.

Again, I want to stress loss aversion is a perfectly normal and healthy bias to have – it is part of our inbuilt defences. Just be conscious of it.

The threat of losing money can be managed in a variety of ways – and I'll be looking at some of these in the chapters that follow. The main point is that taking steps to overcome your fear of losing money has the potential to set you on a very different path – one that can help you achieve financial security and freedom. I'm not saying it never hurts to lose money. Nothing could be further from the truth. But the key is to manage the risk rather than avoid it altogether.

Self-attribution: never wrong, always right

I am sure you know someone (or many people) who has rather high opinions of their opinions – the person who is always right, even when they are wrong. These people tend to have a level of confidence that makes them, in their mind anyway, near invincible. This is a classic description of someone who is overconfident.

Overconfidence leads to self-deception. To protect their ego from the inevitable failure that comes with overconfidence, people will transfer that failure onto someone or something else. This is called self-attribution bias – where people attribute their successes to their personal skills and their failures to factors beyond their control.

This bias is dangerous when money is involved as it leads investors to believe they have more control over their investments than they truly do. Successful investing involves forecasting and in-depth analysis of the future; overconfident investors can overestimate their ability to identify successful investments and invest with 'half knowledge' or limited information, which can lead to mistakes and losses.

Let me give you an example of self-attribution bias in the real world. You may or may not have heard the investment terms 'bulls' and 'bears'. There are many theories as to where these terms originated, but the consensus seems to be that they came from the 'attack' form of each animal. A bull attacks from low to high, whereas a bear attacks from high to low. This is why a market that is rising is described as a bull market, and a market that is falling is described as a bear market. The terms are also used to describe people's views being either positive or negative, which is where self-attribution bias comes in.

The Australian housing market is one of the most debated markets around. It is a market that negative bear investors have targeted time and time again, describing it as 'a bubble', 'fundamentally overvalued', 'a bloodbath waiting to happen' and 'a catastrophic collapse in the making'. Yet every one of these doomsday predictions and analyses has, so far, been wrong.

These bears, in response to being wrong, have come up with a range of external factors to blame: 'the Reserve Bank of Australia has slashed interest rates to keep the party going', 'the politicians need the housing market to remain strong or it would ruin this country' and 'this country remains on the property merry-go-round to its detriment'.

Each quote is an example of people attributing their wrong call to reasons that are outside of their control. However, you watch how fast they are to tell the world they are right when the housing market eventually turns (because it will – all markets experience downturns and housing is no different).

Admitting you're wrong is hard – no doubt – but admitting you are wrong with money is doubly hard. In the Australian housing market example, those quotes I've listed date back as far as 2011. Over the decade 2011 to 2021, the Australian residential housing market rose 84 per cent and the overall housing market 96 per cent.

If the naysaying bears divested from the property market in 2011 and stayed out because they foresaw an ever-present collapse, they will have missed out on their property investment almost doubling. All because of a bias.

It is understandable why investors experience and exhibit this bias. We'll discuss it in more detail in coming chapters, where we'll couple it with identity, which of course can be wrapped up in money: how much you make, how you make it and how you spend it. Money mistakes are materially wrapped up in image.

Heuristic simplification: cutting corners

Behavioural finance and psychologists love a complex buzz term, and there is none better than 'heuristic simplification'.

Heuristics is a blanket term for shortcutting – for example, when people use a 'rule of thumb' in decision-making, especially when they are not sure about something, that is using heuristics.

Humans use heuristics to navigate social and professional situations essentially using their instinct. As we discussed in chapter 1, we instinctively know the norms of the social setting we find themselves in and use the rules of thumb to shape our behaviour to fit in.

For example, if you were to meet the Queen, you would know to be on your best behaviour. When you meet someone new, you talk and act in a different way to when you are catching up with an old friend. These are examples of you using heuristics to simplify your social interactions.

Heuristics are good for human interactions; however, they can be a hindrance in the world of money and investing, where we need to assess high levels of information quickly or when under stress. This can lead to oversimplification or the misuse of information.

There are four parts to heuristic simplification – anchoring, availability bias, attention bias and confirmation bias – and they can all affect how we think and act around money. Note the four parts are not mutually exclusive – they overlap and can work together or against each other.

Anchoring

'First impressions last.' We're all familiar with this phrase and have seen examples of when first impressions have worked, and when they haven't. The first impression gives you a baseline or anchor point to help you decide how you will react to and interact with a person. And, of course, experience shows that first impressions are not always right.

In behavioural finance, the term 'anchoring' describes your first impression of a financial situation. You tend to stick to that first impression – rightly or wrongly. It becomes your reference point, from which you make all future financial judgements.

Let's say for instance that you're in the market for a new car. You find the make and model you're interested in – it's priced at $35,000.

Armed with this benchmark, you start shopping around and find a dealer who agrees to sell you the same make and model for $33,000 – a $2000 discount. Your internal 'anchored' mind sees this as a win and leads you to ink the deal and hand over the cash.

But have you just shortcut your way out of an even better deal?

What if the next dealer offers you the same car for $31,000? What if the better deal was not that car at $35,000 but the car worth $40,000 going for $35,000? Your first impression was that you were being offered a car that was 'cheap', and this stopped you from making a more informed decision by doing more market research.

Price anchoring can also impact your investment decision-making. For example, let's look at a bank stock that is trading at $90 and another bank stock priced at $30. Both banks are well regarded and have strong earnings. Based on this information, many investors will choose the $30 bank share as it appears to be worth the same as the $90 bank share but is cheaper. They are anchored by price, and by the opinion that the $90 share is 'expensive'.

However, this isn't enough information on which to make a sound investment decision.

What I conveniently left out is that the bank with the $30 stock has half the number of customers as the bank with the $90 stock, so it must discount its products to get business. It's also considered fully valued – meaning there's little chance of further short-term growth. The bank with the $90 stock, on the other hand, is continuing to innovate, and business is growing well without having to discount. This stock is considered an investment opportunity.

Now, with that information, your opinion should have been swayed. However, research has found that even with this extra information, many people's initial anchor point, the $90 price, will make them doubt it's a good investment because it still seems 'expensive' compared to the $30 stock.

The final part of the anchoring phenomenon is the round number effect. This is where there is disproportionate level of interest in hitting a round number – for example, when the S&P/ASX 200 index hits 7000 points or the S&P 500 index breaks 4800.

These figures mean very little in the scheme of things, but they anchor people's view and can cause irrational behaviour. It has been suggested that humans like round numbers because we can easily deal with them compared to non-round numbers, and there are several studies that also suggest round numbers are more 'aesthetically pleasing'.

People also tend to round off their savings. Let's say you're saving for a house deposit, your kids' education, a rainy day or, more importantly, your financial freedom.

To reach these goals most people will choose a figure like 'save 5 per cent'. Let's say you are saving 5 per cent of your monthly salary. It's not a huge amount, nor is it too small. We'll assume your salary is $3000 a month, so you are saving $150 a month. You decide to save for 10 years. The average yearly return you get when you invest over those 10 years is 6 per cent – meaning you will have amassed $24,700 after 10 years if all things remain equal.

But why choose 5 per cent? Why not 6 or even 7 per cent? A small percentage increase can have a huge impact on your future, possibly without much additional short-term pain.

If we take the same example and assumptions and apply a savings rate of 6 and 7 per cent, you will have amassed $29,600 at 6 per cent ($180 a month), or $34,600 at 7 per cent ($210 a month). You could be 20 per cent better off if you save 6 per cent, or 40 per cent better off with 7 per cent.

So, why do we round? A 2013 study into the rounding effect found that consumers like to round the cost of their purchases when they are buying fuel at personally operated petrol pumps. The conclusions from the study were that rounded numbers are easier to remember, process and perform mathematics on. The number five is much easier to work with than six or seven.

It's just another example of us using simple shortcuts to make our daily lives easier – heuristic simplification.

Availability bias

There can't be too many of us who haven't daydreamed about how we'd spend a major lottery win. The daydream is so tantalising that, according to the Australian Institute of Health and Welfare, one in three Australians gambles regularly, with lottery games attracting the biggest number of participants.

Common sense tells us the odds are stacked against us. The chance of winning the Powerball lottery is miniscule – you're looking at odds of one in 134 million. Obviously, that's not a great marketing point.

Instead, companies that rely on gambling revenue tap into availability bias to encourage us to believe we can be the next winner. In essence, availability bias means our perception about the likelihood of something happening depends on information that comes readily to mind (see figure 3.1). It's a close cousin of recency bias, where we see positive or negative recent events as the most likely long-term outcome. So, if we see a story about someone winning big on lotto, that will alter our perception of the likelihood we will win – despite any evidence of poor odds we may have encountered previously.

Figure 3.1: Availability bias

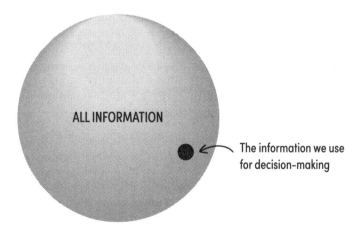

ALL INFORMATION

The information we use
for decision-making

If we see news of a major aviation disaster, we think twice about getting on a flight for fear our plane could be the next to crash. Look more closely and we can identify that this thought process is irrational – the odds of dying as a commercial airline passenger are about one in 205,552, according to the US National Safety Council. Compare that to a one in 2745 chance of choking to death on a piece of food, an action you wouldn't give a second thought to. But when you combine those statistics, think about this: you're more likely to be killed by the peanuts the flight attendant hands out with your drink than the plane having an accident.

Availability bias also kicks in when we encounter good news stories – such as the earlier lotto example. It changes our views about the odds, encouraging us to think that, yes, it must be our turn to come up with the winning numbers. Casinos have mastered the art of playing on availability bias. You'll often see news of the latest big winners promoted near the front entrance. On a smaller scale, next time you're heading into a pub or gaming room, take a look at the keno sign in the bar area – there is a fair chance the display will list the value of the most recent big win. What we never hear about are the millions of people who've lost money on the lottery or any other form of gambling – which is just the way these organisations like it.

Availability bias doesn't just impact gambling. It also impacts investment decisions. Let's take the rise of investment options like meme stocks or cryptocurrencies. The information on each is limited. When information is provided, it's filled with stories of huge windfalls claiming it is the future of finance and money.

What is so concerning about these examples is that a lot of the immediate information is true. People have made fortunes on meme stocks and some people have become millionaires a hundred times over through crypto. However, these people are the exception, not the rule. Meme stocks, crypto and the like are the perfect examples of how our biases, coupled with your personality traits, can lead to detrimental investment behaviours.

'The quick buck effect' is just another way of describing availability bias – both want you to believe you can reach your goals well ahead of time.

Attention bias

That quick buck some are attracted to moves us from availability bias to attention bias.

Numerous behavioural finance studies have found that individual investors are more likely to buy rather than sell things that catch their attention. This is especially true when these shiny things are mentioned in the media, have abnormal amounts of trading volumes or have an extreme one-day move.

The most glaring example of attention bias in recent history was the GameStop saga.

For those who don't have a social media account, TV or Millennial in the family, let me quickly summarise.

At the beginning of 2021, a group of active Reddit users wanted to target several hedge fund managers they saw as 'corrupting the system'. Enter US-based retail video game provider GameStop (GME). GME is a run-of-the-mill sort of company listed on the New York Stock Exchange. Several hedge fund managers believed GME was less than a run-of-the-mill company and decided to 'short' it – that is, they borrowed GME stocks from unit holders and sold these borrowed units in the market. This meant they were betting that the stock price would go down.

However, an army of Reddit users in a forum called r/WallStreet-Bets took issue with this and collectively bought GME stocks over and over – so much so that they started to overrun the hedge funds. This pushed the stock price higher and higher, which in turn forced the hedge fund managers to close their short positions and, in the process, lose a fortune.

It instantly became the biggest financial news story in the world. Day after day for six weeks the GameStop saga was leading global news.

Initially, it was presented as a David versus Goliath affair, but very quickly the media and markets turned their attention to just how much money some traders and investors were making. This is when attention bias started to become a problem, because the initial reason for the GME trade (beating hedge fund managers at their game) was lost in the narrative, and it became a story about the quick buck.

I want to expand on this further, but first let's bring this back to the work of Daniel Kahneman. Kahneman found that attention bias arises particularly on the buy side of investing, because it requires investors to sift through thousands of investment options while being limited by how much information they can process before buying. The sell side of investing doesn't trigger this problem because investors tend to only sell securities they already own, so there's less research involved. Kahneman found that the issue with attention-based purchases is that they can lead to disappointing returns or even loss, as the attention event can be a one-off or a false reason to invest in the first place.

That last sentence perfectly summarises what happened with investors who got caught up in the attention GME was getting. Their attention bias overrode the fact that what was happening was an abnormal event and was no basis for buying GME stocks. Instead, the attention on GME was all the information needed for thousands of investors to buy GME at incredible prices.

The GameStop saga eventually dissipated; the media and market moved on. The attention on the stock drifted and suddenly thousands were stuck with hugely inflated stock holdings in a mediocre company. All because their attention bias overrode their reasoning.

Confirmation bias

We come to our final heuristic: confirmation bias. It has very similar traits to availability and attention bias and plays on your ingrained thinking. As the name suggests, confirmation bias is the phenomenon of seeking selective information to support your own opinions, or interpreting facts in a way that suits your own world view.

When we hold views on things like politics, health, money or any subject for that matter, we actively seek to confirm what we believe through the opinions of friends, colleagues, experts and others. However, this clouds our view. If we only listen to and engage with certain views and information, this limits our ability to make informed decisions.

The echo chambers of social media have turbocharged confirmation bias. It's never been so easy to confirm what you believe – just scroll through your social media feeds and you'll find posts that positively reinforce your choices, beliefs and views. Interact with those posts and the algorithms will suggest other accounts for you to follow that share similar content, reinforcing the echo chamber even further.

Confirmation bias has an added kick in that it plays on the human desire to be right. As a human you will actively avoid critical opinions, reports or information that goes against your point of view. Instead, confirmation bias means you will actively seek opinions, reports and information that paint your points of view in positive light.

Money is far from immune from confirmation bias. Think about it: why is buy now pay later more popular than interest-free payment programs, even though they are essentially the same offering? Because everyone's using buy now pay later. There's no other reason, but your choice has been confirmed as good by those around you.

There are some big financial ideas related to confirmation bias. For example, why haven't cryptocurrencies overtaken fiat currencies in our everyday lives? Why do we think property is a better investment than most other asset classes even though its long-term returns are lower than some asset peers? Because it's worked for others, and that is all the confirmation we need.

There are also plenty of beliefs about money that can contribute to confirmation bias. For example, did you grow up believing that investing is gambling, money is the root of all evil or gold is the only reliable form of currency? You will undoubtably have significant personal bias in the way you respond to these ideas, which in itself should make you sit up and wonder – 'Have I allowed my confirmation bias to cloud my thinking about money?'

Anchoring, availability bias, attention bias and confirmation bias are all examples of how our brain's need to simplify decision-making can really cost us long term. The simple way to counter heuristic simplification is: 'don't judge a book by its cover'. Actively search for differing opinions, views and information. Ask the fundamental question we should all ask ourselves – *is this best option, or do I just think it is?*

Next we'll look at how personality fits with our view on money – and the challenges and pitfalls that can bring.

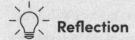 **Reflection**

- Can you identify any of these biases in your own thinking and behaviour around money? (Be honest – there is no judgement here.)
- What might your biases be trying to protect you from?
- What steps could you put in place to help you overcome your vulnerability to the biases you identified?

Chapter 4

The five money personalities

We continue to shape our personality all our life.
If we knew ourselves perfectly, we should die.
– Albert Camus

Knowing who you are means understanding your personality. As philosopher Albert Camus said, knowing yourself is a lifelong journey – and money matters are just part of that journey. However, it's a worthwhile journey to take. Understanding your money personality gives you clues about why your mind reacts the way it does to certain behaviours. The more aware you are of your mind and how it works, the better you can grasp the 'why' behind your behaviours and put steps in place to manage them if necessary.

Relationships have a very interesting part to play in shaping our personality. Humans are social beings – it's in our nature to form strong bonds with others. These bonds of friendship, love and family also flow through to how we manage our own money; our actions with money don't just affect us as individuals. We share our lives with other people – a spouse or partner, our children, friends and family, even workmates. How we handle money can impact the relationships we have with all these people.

We've talked about how our identity, and by extension our personality, is formed through a litany of experiences. A Cambridge University study went further to look at how our family upbringing influences our views about and relationship with money. The research found children's core financial habits are likely formed by the age of seven, and the key driver of this is their parents' money habits – both good and bad.

The Cambridge study noted that young children not only watch their parents with keen interest, but they are also brilliant at imitating their caregivers' behaviours and will do this even later in life. This suggests that one of the best ways to assist our children with money is to understand our own money personality and behaviours, so we can avoid passing bad habits on to our children.

You might also be wondering about nature versus nurture. On this score at least, it seems some of us are more likely to be hardwired to be spenders rather than spendthrifts. A 2017 University of Michigan study found children as young as five can already have distinct emotional reactions to spending relative to the act of saving money. Of course, at age five very few children have had any sort of formal teaching around money matters.

So it's fair to assume the tendency to be more of a spender or a saver comes back to how the adults in a child's life talk (or don't talk) about money, how they react to things like store prices when shopping, and whether money is a source of stress in a household. On the other hand, it could be that we enter the nursery with a 'born to shop' outlook versus an 'I love savings' mentality – but that is clearly hard to prove in children so young.

As an aside, while this type of behavioural research may shed a light on your own money mindset, it also reinforces the value of having relaxed and sensible conversations about money with your kids from a young age. Wait until your children are in their teens and you may have lost a valuable formative decade. As we discussed in chapter 3, bias has a significant impact on money behaviour. One way to help your kids form positive views about money rather than negative views is reinforcing behaviours and experiences that promote better outcomes. It can be as simple as helping your little ones understand the concept of trade by getting them to spend their own 'value' items (such as trading a thing they value for a toy), introducing pocket money or setting up a savings tool like a piggy bank that you add interest to if they hold on to their savings for a period of time. All these actions positively impact kids' view of money and will put them in good stead for the future.

Identifying your money personality

There are lots of different definitions of money personalities. Some say there are seven, some as many as 10, but when you summarise them, there are really four main money personality types and one that could be described as 'ambivalent'. The five money personalities I introduce in this book – the saver, the spender, the debtor, the investor and the ignorer – are based on my observations of the thousands of investors I've worked with.

Of course, we are all too unique to be categorised into just a handful of groupings that accurately describe each of us. Money personality traits are not one-size-fits-all. We won't all fit neatly into a single personality; but you may recognise more of yourself in one personality relative to another. Certain money traits can be more dominant than others.

The point of the exercise is to get to know your strengths and your blind spots. Recognising the way you see money can help you understand why you hold so much or so little in your bank account – and why your mindset can play a big role in your overall financial wellbeing and freedom. It can shed light on why you find it hard to break old spending or saving habits.

So, how do you shape up across the five key money personalities? Let's take a look.

The saver

A work colleague of mine, whom we'll call Anne, perfectly fits the bill as a saver. Her personal motto is 'never pay full price'; she is happy to wait until items are discounted before making a purchase. She is conscious of turning off the lights when leaving a room, always aims to pay for purchases with cash rather than credit, owns her home mortgage free and has very little personal debt.

Anne doesn't regard herself as a cheapskate, but she admits to enjoying having a decent balance of cash sitting in her savings account. She is conservative. While she is happy to grow her superannuation, Anne isn't comfortable taking on high-risk investments, so she leaves her balance in conservative assets – even though she has several decades before she can access her retirement savings.

These are all classic characteristics of a saver. For anyone facing serious debt problems, Anne's situation can seem enviable. The catch is that penny pinching doesn't build wealth, nor does it necessarily mean that Anne has financial choice or freedom.

Anne acknowledges that several good investment opportunities have passed her by because she was too risk averse to dip into her savings to invest in something offering higher returns. She is concerned that she 'could need that money in an emergency'.

She has been unwilling to use debt to improve her home or buy an investment property. She never spends on life experiences like travel or dining out as she doesn't see the value.

Having a saver personality does show that you have discipline and are able to overcome that human trait of wanting an instant return. It also shows suggests you have a strong tendency towards rational financial decision-making.

But it also shows that money itself is of 'physical value' to you, and that parting with it for another asset (an investment, object or experience) makes you feel extremely uncomfortable. The other assets don't have the same worth as the money itself in the saver's eyes. Savers also have a high affinity with loss aversion, which is one of the hardest biases to alter.

If money seems like a physical thing to you, ask yourself why. Understand that the security of having physical money now will impede your ability to grow your funds over time. The money you have today needs to grow as time passes, otherwise it is being eroded by inflation.

No one ever went broke being a saver, and that's good – but savers also miss out on opportunities that would provide them financial choice. My colleague Anne is a long way from struggle street. However, her conservative views around money are probably preventing her from reaching her full financial potential.

The spender

As the name suggests, spenders focus on parting with their cash more than making it work for them. A spender is not just someone who shops till they drop – it's much broader than this.

Spenders generally enjoy the latest of everything – from new tech gadgets to recent home trends, to flash experiences, to expensive things that are of no significant benefit to anyone. All of this costs money, yet none of us have unlimited cash resources to draw on – and this can leave spenders facing some solid debt.

This type of debt is referred to as 'bad debt' – debt on assets that have negative appreciation (such as vehicles, travel or apparel) and high rates of interest (such as personal loans, credit cards and buy now pay later schemes). The asset purchased will depreciate over time to zero. Good debt, on the other hand, is debt used to finance an investment or asset that will appreciate in value faster than the rate of interest.

Spenders can be driven by a variety of different forces. Fear of missing out (FOMO) can be one motivator. This goes back to the stereotypical phrase 'keeping up with the Joneses'. Spenders who are prone to comparing themselves with their peers can find themselves in real financial stress; some may even overextend themselves to the point of bankruptcy. A study by the Federal Reserve Bank Philadelphia found that those living next door to lottery winners are more likely to file for bankruptcy. The reason is thought to be that the lotto-winning neighbour would spend big on a new car, fancy home improvements and other purchases, leading the neighbours who hadn't won the lotto to subconsciously follow suit and spend big on similar items, even though they were not the ones who landed the jackpot. This meant overextending themselves financially and eventually facing bankruptcy.

The emotional satisfaction of spending money can also come into play. A study published in the *Journal of Consumer Psychology* showed that a 'shopper's high' really is a thing. The study found that retail therapy can make us feel happier immediately and help us push through sadness because it gives us a sense of control over our world. But like all highs, the feel-good moment is short-lived. The longer-term legacy for spenders can be a lean bank account, low savings and, worse, over-the-top debt.

Interestingly enough, studies have found that a spender personality is not averse to investing or growing wealth. In fact, spenders are often more comfortable taking on risk than savers. The issue for spenders is that many tend to see investing as something they will get around to eventually – as soon as the latest sale season is done and dusted.

The other reality for spenders is that material possessions tend to lose their lustre quickly, both in terms of the joy they bring and their dollar value. This puts spenders in a money cycle that can quickly get out of control, because they are always looking for new shiny things. Their spending can well and truly outpace their earnings.

Breaking any psychological loop is hard, and spenders should not expect to change their money habits quickly. Instead, thinking of small incremental changes is best. Starting a budget with small additional steps added over time is a good start point; this can help rein in those urges to spend, freeing up cash to pay off credit card or buy now pay later debt, or put more money into your bank account. From there you can get back on track to grow the beginnings of a tidy nest egg to start investing. And who knows? Growing a portfolio could bring much the same dopamine hit as buying that new pair of jeans.

Please also understand that spenders don't have to go cold turkey with their spending. Part of enjoying your money is having the ability to choose what you use it on. It's about making sure you have the money to make a spending choice, rather than being beholden to the negativity of overspending and debt.

The debtor

If you're regularly maxed out on your credit cards, live from pay day to pay day or are juggling multiple personal loans, you may identify with the debtor personality. The common thread that can identify a debtor is that they continually spend more than they earn and use borrowings to sustain that spending. The debtor is similar to the spender, however they are more likely to not just overspend but to use debt in ways that lead to significant financial hardship.

The debt I'm talking about here is depreciating debt – debt used to purchase here-today-gone-tomorrow items of no lasting value. Debt doesn't have to mean an outstanding credit card balance. Increasingly, people are turning to buy now pay later and other 'zero-interest' schemes, which have the potential to leave the unwary in just as much financial pain as high-interest credit cards.

Just like the spender, there can be a variety of reasons why people end up on a never-ending death loop of bad debt. The causes can be as clear as loss of income through illness or injury, or as complex as a gambling addiction. But all lead to long-term financial issues and money cycles that need to be broken.

According to the American Psychology Association, nearly three in every four American couples rate money as the biggest stressor in their relationship, and nearly one in four have suffered extreme stress because of money. The report found that in some cases people even put their healthcare needs on hold due to their finances. The damage the debt cycle can create is extensive.

Most psychologists and money experts agree that the critical first step in breaking the cycle of debt is to understand what drives you to keep overspending. Part of the problem is that debtors don't always pay much attention to their personal finances – and some people can be surprised to learn that not everyone lives with a revolving door of debt.

Getting your debt under control is paramount. Short-term lending products with their very high interest rates are effectively taking upwards of 20 per cent out of your after-tax pay. And of course, the principal amount also needs to be repaid sometime in the future. This is why debtors have huge difficulty getting ahead financially. The key focus should be on bringing debt under control and improving your ability to set aside extra cash for savings – and, from there, for investment.

Help is available if you're struggling with debt. There are free financial counselling services that can help you consolidate your debts and address your relationship with money.

The investor

The investor is someone who has a clear picture of their financial situation and is actively working towards achieving their goals by spending less then they earn, saving the difference and investing those savings.

For investors, sensible money management isn't about being a tightwad or obsessing over money. It's more a case of putting their money to work in a way that matches their goals and appetite for risk. Investors tend to be more assertive than savers and are willing to forgo a level of certainty to get what they want. Investors are also more likely to spend on assets they see as beneficial in the long term, like doing work on an investment property or adding value to their private residence to help it appreciate.

This group tends to be more financially well off. They have more options for financial choice and freedom. However, some can go from investors to debtors quickly if they overleverage themselves on bad investment assets or become overconfident in their abilities, leading to poor investment decisions.

That said, if you do identify as an investor, chances are you're on the right track and you should notch up the benefits over time.

The ignorer

The ignorer, sometimes described as an ostrich, is someone who ignores their personal finances and pleads ignorance about any problems that result. An ignorer will more than likely have no knowledge of their financial position as they won't check their bank balance, credit card statements or retirement account.

This doesn't necessarily mean they don't have money – its more that they are completely nonchalant about their finances. This means they will fail to make long-term investment decisions, let opportunity pass them by and miss out on assets like a family home because they have not accumulated the financial means to buy them.

Fear is a common trait underlying this personality. Anxiety about making a decision can lead to no choices being made at all. This can feel like the easier option rather than making a decision that turns out to be 'wrong'.

Having an ignorer personality can also lead to personal finance decisions being delegated out. This is where the person hands over their financial decision-making to a partner, peer or adviser, with no idea what they are invested in or how their money is being used by the delegated party.

If you're an ignorer, the first step to combat this is to find a way to move past fear and engage with your finances. This can be as simple as finding out where your income lands. Is it in a certain bank account, or multiple accounts? From there, start to look at your outgoings. What are you spending on? Where is your money going? Having this knowledge can be the first step in you becoming more organised and aware of your money. From there, look to start a goal-orientated savings plan. It can be as simple as saving for a night out, then building from there – a holiday, a house deposit, retirement savings and so on.

Can you change your money personality?

Once you determine which of these personality types describes you best, it's worth drawing up an action plan to bring about change. Small, incremental changes in the way we deal with our finances are a lot easier to implement than drastic changes. Small changes also have the potential to yield big results over time.

You might wonder if it is possible to change your money personality. I'm not sure it's possible to entirely change your personality, but we do evolve. Acknowledging who and what you are will help you address the financial hurdles your personality type can encounter. Getting to know yourself better isn't always easy. Making change can be even harder. But if your money personality is the thing that's holding back your financial wellbeing, it's worth the effort.

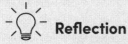 **Reflection**

· Which money personality do you most identify with?
· What are some of the financial hurdles you struggle with related to your money personality?
· What small, incremental changes could you introduce to address these hurdles?

Chapter 5

When money collides

There are people who have money and people who are rich.
– Coco Chanel

If personality is what makes you *you*, it is also what makes everyone else *them*. The interaction of personalities is one of the most fascinating topics you can read about. Under research conditions, human relations often seem completely irrational, yet in the real world they work through adaption, change and desire.

Relationships are complicated because they are entangled in our personal needs and desires. Cold hard rationale is very unlikely to be involved in anyone's choice of partner. It is one of those great wonders of life: how two people who have different personalities, biases, cultural considerations and learned experiences can be drawn together. The debate about biology sometimes enters the discussion as viewed from physical anthropology, and there's a social anthropology idea that we 'settle' in our choice of partners because of ease, time and the want to settle down.

The most interesting factor to me is how we meet our partners, and the chances of each pair finding each other. When you think about that, it's staggering.

Let's go back to the university lecture where we found out our brains are physiologically the same as those who were born more than 35,000 years ago. Our lecturer's next trick was to pose this question: on a sliding scale, what is the probability of finding a mate in this world? He drew a long, continuous line on the board and asked us all to put a dot where we thought the probability sat. Most of us followed the bell curve idea and landed somewhere in the middle. The lecturer smiled, and then put down his dot.

It was at the very start of the line – a probability of 0.005 per cent, or 'statistically impossible'.

Here was his rational reasoning. There are 8 billion people in the world. Roughly half are male, half are female. That cuts your options in half immediately, even for those attracted to people of the same sex. Of the 4 billion people left, 95 per cent are likely to be outside your age bracket – that is, they are either going to be too old or too young for you. So, now you are down to 200 million, which is still a lot. Then you look at geography – of that 200 million, how many live within a distance of 10 kilometres?

Why 10 kilometres? We need to be able to physically interact with our partners easily. Living far apart makes interactions limited – not impossible, clearly, but we don't like delayed returns and that includes where physical interaction is concerned.

That 200 million has now been whittled down to just several thousand.

This is where chance comes into it. How do you actually meet these people? Through friends, family, a chance meeting, going to school together, in the workplace or via a dating app? All these are chance encounters. And when you do meet these people, are you physically attracted to them? Remember, this is a physical anthropological perspective, so shallowness is allowed. Do you interact with the other person, or do you miss your chance to connect? Finally, what are the chances your personalities are compatible?

Hence the lecturer's 0.005 per cent dot. Under the physical anthropology theory, our ability to find a mate is near impossible because of the physical world. Yet, we do meet partners, and it's because we want it to happen – it's as simple as that. Our biology and our desire to procreate will compel us to meet and form a relationship with someone in our sphere. The lesson from my physical anthropology lecture was that it is almost certain you will have differences, but you will find a partner.

The relationship pressure cooker

The beauty of having a relationship is sharing your life with someone; enjoying a lifestyle and having adventures; experiencing success and failures; making memories and sharing dreams. These are all actions that have personal value, but they don't necessarily have the possibility of value differences or a loss of value.

Financial transactions, borrowing money, earning differences, spending, saving, betting, investing in relationships – these do have loss attached, because while you might not see any issues with spending or borrowing, your partner might.

We all know that couples have differences. Every couple faces challenges and disagreements from time to time, sometimes leading to bickering and arguments. Add money to those challenges and you add a pressure that can be visceral, because money has deep-seated psychology attached to it.

Research shows that fights over money are the second most common cause of divorce in the US, behind infidelity. In Australia, one in four people say money has created a sense of imbalance in their relationship, while one in five admit they have had past relationships that ended because of money problems.

Certain money behaviours are particular turn-offs that can see a relationship end before it even gets off the ground. A recent survey identified the main behaviours that people won't put up with in their romantic interest (see table 5.1). Top of the list is 'destructive spending' – that is, excessive spending on things like gambling, smoking and alcohol. That is followed by lying about your financial situation, then struggling to pay for the basics or relying heavily on credit.

Table 5.1: Top financial relationship dealbreakers

Destructive spending	80.2%
Lying about their financial situation	76.8%
Inability to pay for basic expenses	71.1%
Putting everything on credit	62.2%
Inability to budget	58.4%
Lack of financial independence	55.7%
No financial plan or goals	52.6%

Source: Kelly Emmerton 2018, 'It's not you, it's your bank account: Australia's biggest financial relationship deal breakers', Mozo, mozo.com.au/personal-loans/articles/biggest-financial-relationship-deal-breakers.

Communication is key

You'll recall from chapter 4 that there are five distinct money person-alities – spenders, savers, debtors, investors and ignorers. It may seem rather obvious that conflict could arise if two people in a relationship have different money personalities. A spender coupled with a saver, for example, may sound like a recipe for disaster. But, like all things in relationships, communication can help smooth any difficulties related to different money personalities.

A US survey found that 94 per cent of respondents who describe their marriage as 'great' said they discuss their money dreams with their spouse, compared to only 45 per cent of respondents who describe their marriage as 'okay' or 'in crisis'. Most of those who reported having a great marriage (87 per cent) also said they and their spouse work together to set long-term goals for their money.

The takeout from this survey is that you and your partner don't need to have identical money personalities to enjoy a lasting relationship. But you *do* need to work as a team, and this inevitably calls for you to be able to discuss money in a constructive, non-judgemental way. Identifying your own – and your other half's – money personality and attitudes to money management is still something that's worth doing, even in the early stages of a relationship. You'll be better able to understand each other's perspective and have constructive conversations that support your relationship, rather than letting money issues fester.

The trouble is that money can be a notoriously difficult subject to raise, even with your long-term partner. Personal finance is something we rarely bring up until we are well into a relationship (if at all), and that's understandable. Conversations around retirement savings or car loans are hardly the stuff of romance.

A lot of us also have deep shame over how we handle money. For example, having to tell your spouse or partner you are in debt or have suffered from financial loss is one of the hardest things you'll experience. The mental strain of knowing your past decisions don't just affect you anymore but also someone (or a group of people) you love can be completely debilitating. It is also one of the leading causes of further loss. The desire to get out of financial strain can lead to further risk-taking behaviour, which inevitably leads to further loss. It is the collision of your money personality and personal desires – the fear your partner will see you as undesirable and no longer an equal in the relationship causes you to want to patch up your mistakes as quickly as possible.

Broaching this subject can also be difficult as it goes against cultural and social norms, where talking about an individual's financial position is seen as a no-no.

But it's worth pushing through your discomfort. Approaching your partner in a non-judgemental way so you can understand why they behave the way they do with money is the best tactic. Be open about your own experiences and challenges with money, too. You could ask your partner what their parents were like with money, as well as their close friends and extended family. Did they overspend? Or were they tight with their money to the extent that they didn't share it?

Share your goals for the future with your partner, and ask them about theirs. Perhaps discuss how you believe you can reach those goals.

Maybe each of you can then share your personal fears around money, and swing the conversation towards strategies that can help both of you allay concerns by taking a proactive approach to your combined finances.

The main point is that whether you've been in the relationship for five months or five years, it is never too early or too late to begin weaving money into conversations. Take it slow, keep it positive, and you could pave the way for further healthy discussions about your finances in the future.

It is important to bear in mind in these conversations that no one has perfect money habits. We all have occasional spending lapses. I'm sure none of us can claim never to have forgotten a bill or bought something we didn't need. There is no shortage of people who have made at least one dud investment decision in their lifetime – I definitely have. So, no matter whether you are a saver, spender, debtor, investor or ignorer, chances are your other half's money personality could bring some fresh strings to your own financial bow.

Yours, mine, ours – have some 'me' space

Being part of a couple doesn't mean having to share absolutely everything. A generation ago it was common for couples to have just one joint bank account where they pooled all their resources. These days, less than one in two (44 per cent) of Australians are happy to share 100 per cent of their finances with their significant other. One in three have some shared finances but maintain a separate bank account with independent funds. One in five Australians choose to keep their finances totally separate from their partner. And most maintain individual superannuation accounts.

Clearly, there is no single right or wrong way for couples to manage their money, regardless of their money personality. Nonetheless, something I have seen work well with my clients is the idea of a 'me' account: an account or savings vehicle where you hold an amount of funds for no-questions-asked personal use. So, if you want to buy a new set of golf clubs (or whatever else interests you), you can. The idea is that the funds in that account are yours to spend, and you can be secure in the knowledge that doing so won't affect your partner, family or overall wealth.

It's wise to offer your partner a similar setting – 'their' account. This way there is less cause for resentment – something that can easily happen if one person is a spender and the other a saver. The other plus of each person having an account they can spend from independently is that it can help to avoid 'financial infidelity'. Financial infidelity is using joint monies on secret or destructive spending. It can also involve having bank accounts or credit cards your other half simply doesn't know about but is liable for as a joint holder. This can occur through loans being taken out on joint assets like the home or the family car. It can also occur if one partner is an 'ignorer' and doesn't ask what the credit is for or why they need it in the first place.

Financial infidelity, for some, can be regarded as worse than an affair. Surveys have shown that as many as one in five think this way. The core reasoning for this belief is the breach of trust, and the hardship it can create – the loss of financial freedom. It's the feeling of having 'lost time'; that the time, effort and sacrifice it took to reach a certain financial position prior to the financial infidelity has now been lost. And then there's the future work required to recover from the situation to consider.

You need to be transparent about money with your partner, especially if your finances are combined.

Play to your strengths

There are clear positives to having differing personalities. You perceive things one way, your partner another, and this gives both of you unique insights: your personal perception can help them see a different view, and vice versa. It also allows you both to play to your strengths.

Couples often tend to delegate tasks, even if this is implicit rather than spelled out. For example, one person may take care of the outside of the dwelling, while the other may manage parts of the inside. One might take responsibility for shopping for groceries, while the other cooks. The same goes with finances: when you know each other's money strengths, you can put your different financial leanings to work to achieve the best possible outcomes.

In a household shared by a saver and a spender, for example, it can work if the spender makes the purchases, researching the best available prices and completing the sales. This can satisfy their inner spending tendencies. The saver, on the other hand, can act as a sounding board, negotiating with their partner to set a budget for the purchase and determining the best way to pay – savings or credit.

Alternatively, you may choose to share roles equally. It's all about what works for you as a couple. One thing I would stress is the value of both parties remaining engaged with the household finances at every stage. That doesn't have to mean you both know the exact date the car insurance is due, or that you both track the value of your investments daily. But it does mean you both show an interest in your financial wellbeing as a couple.

The reason I say this is because relationship breakdown is a fact of modern life. Australian Bureau of Statistics figures show that in 2020, 78,989 couples married, while 49,510 divorced. This suggests that more than one in two marriages will not last the full distance. Staying in touch with the household finances while you're part of a couple can mean fewer unpleasant surprises if things don't go well and you decide to separate in the future.

The collision of money in a relationship is clearly a large stressor. But drill down deeper, and the real issue may not be money at all. Relationships Australia makes the point that while plenty of research suggests money and finances can impact the quality of a relationship, it may just be the symptom, rather than the cause.

It is always worth trying to understand your different perspectives and hopefully reach a middle ground you can both agree on – regardless of your money personalities.

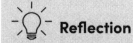 **Reflection**

- Which money personality does your partner most identify with?
- How might you and your partner support each other's strengths and weaknesses when it comes to money?
- When was the last time you had a calm, non-judgemental conversation about money with your partner? Are you both clear on your money goals as a couple and individually?

Chapter 6

Liberation: the reality of choice

Destiny is no matter of chance. It is a matter of choice. It is not a thing to be waited for, it is a thing to be achieved.
– William Jennings Bryan

If I were to ask what makes you happy, I suspect your initial reaction would be to pause and reflect. Because what does make you happy... really? It's a more complex question than it might seem. Chances are, it's not going to be possessions or your work or your wealth, even if these things may or may not define part of your personality.

According to the *Journal of Personality and Social Psychology*, the number-one contributor to happiness is *autonomy*; that is, 'The feeling that your life – its activities and habits – are self-chosen and self-endorsed.'

The person behind this line of thinking was American psychologist Angus Campbell. He said: 'Having a strong sense of controlling one's life is a more dependable predictor of positive feelings of wellbeing than any of the objective conditions of life we have considered.'

Study after study has found that those who believe they have control of their personal destiny report having 'extraordinary positive feelings of happiness'.

Being in control of your destiny is subjective. Let me tell you about my personal experience of losing control, where money fitted in and my 'liberation'.

My personality and persona has always been interwoven with my success. In the past, particularly, I have defined myself by my success. I am not ashamed to say this as I know this to be true – at least, I do now.

I first realised this when I was forced to stop and evaluate my happiness (or lack of it) when my success, personal control and wellbeing collided. At the time, I was working in an area I loved (and still do): living in the world markets. My job involved researching, writing about, talking about, presenting on and investing in markets. It was a career I had never in my wildest dreams believed I could have; nor did I realise it would be so fulfilling. With that level of satisfaction, my ability to do what was required came naturally – and so did success.

However, while I loved what I did, the working environment I was in was suboptimal. I had no control over my time, my direction, my position or my internal success. It was clear I was disposable, that nothing was ever good enough and that my value to the organisation was low. No amount of fulfilment can overcome this kind of situation, and I began to loathe going to work.

Loathing something I had previously loved was one of the hardest things to reconcile, but I knew why I was feeling that way – I had lost control of my destiny. What I didn't know was how to get it back.

I am very fortunate to have people I can lean on and consult, and after a very constructive discussion with my uncle (a psychologist and counsellor), we mapped out a plan for getting my control back. It looked like this

1. **Know it will end** – Although I couldn't see a way out of my situation, understanding it wasn't forever and that it would eventually end was the first step. In essence I had to accept the current situation while also knowing it wouldn't always be that way.

2. **Find a dealing mechanism** – I then had to step back, look at what I needed and what my mind needed to accept so my current reality wouldn't affect my thinking or mindset going forward. For me that mechanism was to disassociate from the culture and intraday mechanics of that workplace. I did what was required during the workday then immediately disengaged once the workday was over – I had no contact at all with work outside work hours. That meant I still had hours in the day for me, and that time I had control over.

3. **Jump on the change** – When change happened, I had to embrace the short-term chaos. I had to accept that my ego would be dented by the perceived loss of success. That loss of success was leaving a career I loved – I didn't know if I would get it back. It was also financial because I lost a stable, well-paying job. It meant going back to square one. What was really happening was I was reshaping my future success, as I could now map out my destiny, control it and liberate my future happiness.

One reason I couldn't see my way out of the situation before that conversation with my uncle was my financial situation. I was making good money and I had family responsibilities, and I didn't want to risk losing that security (loss aversion bias comes in many forms; this was mine).

Once I was out on my own, however, the true value of money and financial freedom became most apparent.

As I had been saving and investing for several years at that point, the financial pressure I thought we were under didn't actually exist. It turned out I had the financial freedom to choose my future and decide on my own path to the personal success I wanted.

It was a liberating realisation.

Our financial position had given me time – time to find fulfilment and redefine success, and by extension my persona and personality. The opportunity to become independent – autonomous, if you will – was life-changing.

There is no greater dividend or investment return than financial freedom. It doesn't matter how much you have, as long as it gives you the ability to do what makes you happy at a time you want, in the way you want. Financial freedom not only liberates you but those dearest to you, as your personal destiny will bring happiness to you and by extension those in your personal sphere.

Time is money; money is time

One way to liberate your financial freedom is to understand what money is, and what it is not. Fundamentally money is just a transfer of value, and in my view, value is in the eye of the beholder.

Thus, value can be anything. Yes, it can be that house or car or holiday or dinner out with a loved one. But it can also be time – as I just showed in my own example. Money can give you time to write that book, change your career or do more of the things you want.

Warren Buffett said of time: 'It's the only thing you can't buy. I mean, I can buy anything I want basically but I can't buy time.' I think he was right in that you can't buy time in terms of slowing down the clock, but you can 'gain time' with money – that is its core value.

The aphorism 'time is money' speaks to the monetary cost of idleness – that is, the more time you're working, the more money you'll make. But maybe 'money is time' is also true. I'll let you ponder that one.

Understanding how you can create your own financial freedom requires having a perceptive on now, tomorrow and the years to come. The story of the Mexican fisherman illustrates this perfectly. Here's how it goes.

An American businessman was at the pier of a small coastal village in Mexico when a small boat with just one fisherman docked. Inside the boat were several large fish. The American complimented the Mexican on the quality of his fish and asked how long it took to catch them.

The Mexican replied, 'Only a little while.' The American then asked why he didn't stay out longer and catch more fish. The Mexican said he had enough to support his family's immediate needs. The American then asked, 'But what do you do with the rest of your time?'

The Mexican fisherman said, 'I sleep late, fish a little, play with my children, take siestas with my wife, Maria, and stroll into the village each evening where I sip wine and play guitar with my amigos. I have a full and busy life.'

The American scoffed, 'I'm a successful businessman and could help you. If you spent more time fishing, you could use the proceeds to buy a bigger boat. With the proceeds from the bigger boat, you could buy several boats; eventually you would have a fleet of fishing boats. Instead of selling your catch to a middleman, you could sell directly to the processor, eventually opening your own cannery. You would control the product, processing and distribution. Of course, you would need to leave this small coastal fishing village and move to Mexico City, then eventually New York City, where you would run your expanding enterprise. In 15 to 20 years, when the time is right, you would announce an IPO, sell your company stock to the public and make millions!'

'Millions,' the Mexican said. 'Then what?'

The American said, 'Then you would retire and move to a small coastal fishing village, where you would sleep late, fish a little, play with your kids, take siestas with your wife and stroll to the village in the evenings, where you could sip wine and play your guitar with your amigos.'

There are many lessons to take from the Mexican fisherman. Less is more; simplify your life; find out what's important to you; direct your time and energy to what matters most; and work to live, rather than living to work. All of these are hugely important in liberating your time.

However, I think something that is lost in this proverb is the thought process around time horizons.

The fisherman is thinking about now, while the banker is thinking way off into the future. Both actually have a part to play in achieving financial freedom. The question is: how can you set up your money to serve you now, tomorrow and years from now?

The bucket strategy

In 1985 US financial planner Harold Evensky developed what is known as the 'bucket strategy'. He intended it to be used mainly by retirees, but anyone at any stage can benefit if they apply it to their whole wealth position.

The idea is to divide your portfolio/wealth into three 'buckets': a cash bucket to use for your living expenses; a shorter-term investment bucket backed by income assets; and a longer-term investment bucket aimed towards growth investments.

A benefit of this approach is it sidelines your psychological biases and ensures your money is working for you over time. By separating your wealth into three clear buckets, you can 'gain time' with cash that covers the now. You also have investments that are generating some income that can be used in the near future, and another set of investments that are set to growth for those longer-term financial freedom goals.

Evensky's idea was that the income produced from buckets two and three could trickle down into the first bucket. Any shortfall could be replenished either systematically on a set schedule or opportunistically during the market's good times. The benefit of this approach is that you can avoid having to sell your portfolio when the market is down, or to meet regular living expenses.

Superannuation and pension funds the world over now offer this set-up for people entering pension phase so their retirement savings are smoothed out over their retirement. However, I think there is an even better way to look at the bucket strategy that makes it suitable for everyone, not just retirees.

I believe the bucket strategy can help us conceptualise our finances in terms of time. As we discussed earlier in the book, our minds like to compartmentalise and will do what they can to ensure quick and easy decision-making. Giving your mind a time continuum will free up your money, free up what's important to you and free up your time.

Let's say you're planning a renovation. You have a builder lined up and they offer you a fixed-price contract at $250,000. Your mind's initial reaction will be, 'I need $250,000 now. Can I do that?' In fact, the contract shows the works will take a year to complete and your payments will only be due on completion of each of five stages.

You will pay $50,000 at the end of each stage, with the last $50,000 due in a year. It's still a $250,000 renovation, but you have time to pay for it in more manageable chunks.

We have a strange habit of looking at money in compartmentalised ways rather than as a whole. We should be viewing our money position as a whole, knowing what that means for our financial wellbeing and freedom – more on that in chapter 10.

Let's now break down Evensky's buckets to see how they can work no matter what stage of life you're in.

Today money

This is the money that comes in from your employment/career – the money you live on, which sits in a bank account you use every day. It's the money that you will be most sensitive to, as it is the most 'fluid' – it comes in, goes out, is spent on here-and-now things and pays the bills that are part of life. When you don't track your today money, it's hard to work out whether you saved some of the money coming in or spent it all.

Evensky's idea was that you need two to three years' worth of cash in this bucket, but that is because the retirees he created the model for don't have an income. What is more important for those still earning is making sure your today money bucket is net positive or able to cover your normal expenses.

I am not saying your bucket needs to be net positive every month or pay cheque, as everyone will have one-offs and unforeseen events. On average, though, you should have a net gain from your income. This gain can then be added to your other buckets: tomorrow money and beyond money.

Today money is about knowing you have enough to live on, enough to pay the bills and enough to go towards your financial future. In short, it should help you sleep at night.

Tomorrow money

This is the money that you may need in two to five years' time – and even then, you might not actually use it, but it's there. It's the money that starts to give you 'time' for that holiday, that house deposit, that break from your career, that time you want to write a book.

This money should be invested into stable assets with a higher income orientation – things that actually earn you money, like term deposits, dividend-paying shares, fixed interest and the like. By having tomorrow's money in a specific bucket, your mind can start to see that, like you paying your builder progressively during the year you have employed them, you have money spread neatly over time: money for now, money for later.

Tomorrow is always coming. It could be tomorrow, it could be in a year, or it might not come for several years – but know that your 'tomorrow money' is waiting for whenever tomorrow might be.

Beyond money

This is the hardest bucket for most people to get their heads around. We humans don't like thinking too far into the future. The thing is, though, when you actually start to think about what the beyond fund is for, you should experience some comfort that you have actually started contributing to it.

Beyond money includes your superannuation and pension savings, the money you put aside for your children and/or grandchildren, the equity in your home, that share portfolio you started – really, its all the assets that you are likely to hold for at least seven years.

This bucket is the one most likely to experience some loss at times, as the money in this bucket should be allocated to growth assets. This is the bucket that will give you the financial freedom you are looking for, and shows that the businessman in the Mexican fisherman story was partially right – you will have wealth when you need it if you think of the future.

The buckets system will set you up so that your money is ready to gain you time. It is with you today, working for tomorrow and growing into the beyond.

Having the ability to see how your money is working for you across time will give you the feeling described in the *Journal of Personality and Social Psychology* – 'The feeling that your life – its activities and habits – are self-chosen and self-endorsed.'

In other words – *financial autonomy.*

The other advantage of ordering your financial time horizons is that time also works for you in another way. Let's discuss that now.

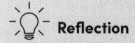 **Reflection**

- How might money create time in your life?
- What lessons do you take from the Mexican fisherman story?
- What steps could you take to start thinking of your money over time, and give yourself financial autonomy?

Chapter 7

Time heals all

The two most powerful warriors are patience and time.
– Leo Tolstoy, *War and Peace*

For human beings, time is a significant force. It dictates our daily movements; it provides a measure of achievement; and it plays havoc with our patience. As discussed in chapter 6, time is one of the greatest things you can gain from financial freedom.

Time also plays an essential role in investment. It can play a leading hand in shaping your returns.

Yet many of us have an uneasy relationship with time. 'The year has flown past!' is a common expression. That's despite time moving at a fixed pace – no matter where you are in the world, and no matter which life stage you are in.

Patience is not something we are renowned for. As we learned in chapter 1, humans haven't psychologically adapted to the modern reality of making decisions today that deliver results over time.

This brings us to the next step in reshaping our mind to overcome the headwinds money can present. We must work out what will get our minds to accept delayed returns.

Delayed returns and discounting

What amount of return would entice you to wait, rather than just accepting what you have now?

Let's start with how classic economics views this question. It refers to it as discounting: we 'discount' a future reward by a fixed percentage for each unit of time we must wait. What this is essentially saying is that if someone has a 'discount' rate of 20 per cent, for example, they should be happy to take $100 now and $120 in a year from now. Furthermore, that same person should be equally happy to receive $100 a year from now and $120 two years from now. This is referred to as 'exponential discounting'. It assumes the amount you discount a future reward today is only dependent on the length of time you have to wait – the discount rate is constant. According to economics there are no ifs, buts or maybes here – and don't even think about considering changing the world in which we live over that time, because economics thinks in a linear fashion.

There is something very *rational* about this view. Yet as we know, humans are not rational – we are reasonable, functional and practical. We are always looking both at the now and the future, and our 'immediate return' minds don't see this idea of linear discounting as very appealing. This has been backed up by swathes of research that suggest people's choices and future discount returns are far from rational. In fact, people have much higher discount rates the *shorter* the wait, which is not what you would expect.

In essence, if you could have $100 today or $110 tomorrow you will more than likely take the $100 today, because why wait a day for an extra $10? But if you could receive $100 in 30 days or $110 in 31 days, you will more than likely wait that one extra day for the larger return – 'I can wait a little longer; it's just an extra day.' However, this is where it gets interesting, because humans are impulsive. If we look at the $100 example again, yes, we are willing to wait that extra day in a month's time. But once the month has passed and we are offered $100 today or a $110 tomorrow, most people will revert to taking the money early.

This behavioural phenomenon is called 'hyperbolic discounting', and it's another psychological bias we all possess.

What hyperbolic discounting suggests is that we are impulsive in the short term but exhibit patience in the long term.

The term was originally coined by American psychologist Richard Herrnstein. His research found the rate at which people discount future rewards declines as the length of the delay increases in a hyperbolic fashion, which means it looks something like figure 7.1.

Figure 7.1: Hyperbolic discounting

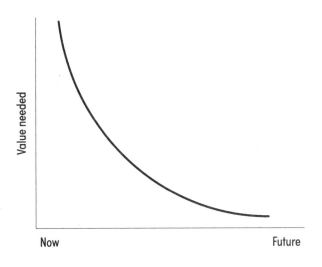

When you think about it, hyperbolic discounting illustrates why it is so easy for us to fall into money traps. Our preference to value immediate return is a blend of human impulses – we are naturally risk averse and naturally impatient.

Human impatience goes a long way to explain the financial success of short-term personal credit payment systems like zero-interest schemes and buy now pay later. There's no certainty that an item on sale today will still be available tomorrow – and who wants to wait to 'save' the purchase price, anyway?

There is another way to look at hyperbolic discounting: through the perspective of delayed returns. That is, we are physiologically geared towards *now*, and having to wait for an additional reward is completely against our make-up. However, hyperbolic discounting also suggests we can see the *value* of taking a long-term approach to money that has a reward – that is, investing.

American economist David Laibson used the concept of hyperbolic discounting to rationalise why we can have large credit card or personal loan balances with high interest rates while simultaneously having pre-retirement wealth (superannuation) growing at lower interest rates.

His research showed that this is because in our minds retirement is a long way away. Even those close to retirement age (due to retire within five years) view it as a long way off according to recent surveys and studies that have been built based on Laibson's findings. Hence, we are happy with a smaller discount reward because we'll be accessing the money so far into the future.

This is rather interesting when you think about it. Maybe my earlier statement needs to be reworded: humans are naturally *short-term* impatient, but *long-term* patient.

From an investment and financial freedom perspective, this is a hugely exciting idea – it suggests that there is a point at which we will take investment over instant reward. It also shows that we recognise that the future rewards we need can be realistic – and, most importantly, achievable – if we are patient.

Math-a-mechanics

Let's look at time in terms of investment, money and debt to see how they relate.

There's a common expression in investment circles: *it's time in the market, not timing the market.*

This is a shorthand way of pointing out that time in the market is more effective at building wealth than trying to time markets. Market research shows that the longer you invest for, the more you benefit from compounding returns versus timing your investments, where you buy and sell the market at times you believe are best – meaning there are periods you are not in the market at all.

If there is only one piece of high school maths you should take with you for life, it is the power of compound interest. No other concept will have such a direct impact on your financial wellbeing and financial freedom as compounding.

Here is the technical difference between simple and compound interest: simple interest is calculated on the principal amount you have invested. Compound interest, on the other hand, is calculated on the principal amount plus the accumulated interest of the previous periods.

Here's how it looks as a formula:

$$A = P\,(1 + r/n)^{nt}$$

A = final amount, P = Principal amount, r = interest rate,
n = number of times the interest is applied per time period,
t = number of time periods elapsed

I know the formula won't resonate in your mind, but the chart of compound interest will (see figure 7.2).

Figure 7.2: Simple versus compound interest

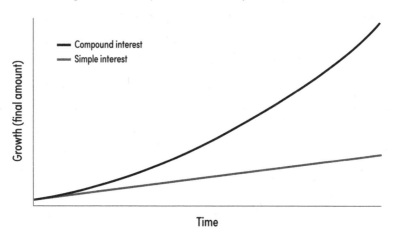

Let's look at an example. Assume you have made an initial investment of $10,000 (you can choose any amount, but obviously the larger your initial investment the faster it will grow). You add nothing more to this investment over the years that follow, other than the annual returns – you don't tip in any more, and nor do you withdraw any money.

Let's assume an annual return of 5 per cent. By the end of year 10, compounding will have seen your investment grow to $16,289. By the end of year 30, it will have increased to $43,219.

Table 7.1: Compounding returns – $10,000 invested for 30 years at 5 per cent annual return

Year	Principal at start of year	Year-end balance
1	$10,000	$10,500
2	$10,500	$11,025
3	$11,025	$11,576
10	$15,513	$16,289
20	$25,270	$25,533
30	$41,161	$43,219

Sticking with the same example, we can see in the diagram below that compounding is slow to start out. Over time, though, the effects can be impressive as compounding begins to dramatically accelerate. By year 15, for instance, the returns to date have totalled $20,789, which is more than double your initial investment. By the end of year 30, you have accumulated $43,219, but your overall return is a massive $33,219 meaning you have lapped your initial $10,000 investment several times over – all by just waiting and letting compound interest do its thing.

Figure 7.3: Compounding returns – $10,000 invested for 30 years at 5 per cent annual return

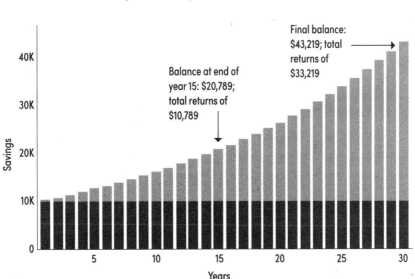

The value of compounding is indisputable. It's something Albert Einstein is credited with describing as 'the eighth wonder of the world – and the most powerful force in the universe'.

I'm fairly certain plenty of astrophysicists would argue that gravity is a far more powerful force, but to give Einstein his due – when it comes to investing, compounding certainly makes a significant difference. Some of the greatest investors in the world use it to great effect – none more so than the pinnacle compound investor Warren Buffett. Figure 7.4 is a chart of Buffett's personal wealth over his lifetime. You'll notice the majority of the growth has occurred towards the latter part of the time period. Buffett is now in his 90s; he started investing at the age of 14.

Figure 7.4: Warren Buffett's net worth by age

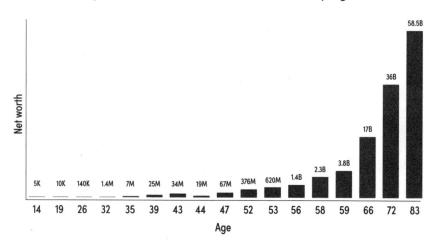

Buffett is exceptional at what he does, so much so that he is one of the most studied financial figures of all time. His messaging is simple and his investment ethos one that millions of people try to replicate.

His core strategy and philosophy is that you should not be concerned with what someone thinks the markets could do; rather, you should be focused on what a *company* (stock) could do. This is because no one can accurately predict markets. If you concentrate on the company's progress, how it operates and its domination over peers, you will be able to hold it for the long term. This has proven to be a winning strategy time after time.

I should be clear here that Buffett's investment journey is that of an institution, not a regular investor. That said, Buffett's investment company Berkshire Hathaway is simply an extension of Buffett's investment method, and millions of investors buy Berkshire Hathaway stocks for this reason. In complete honesty, I too think Buffett is someone to admire and study.

However, it's important to be careful if you find yourself idolising someone like Buffett. In chapter 1 we talked about icons in history: Plato, Newton, Einstein and so on. These people are exceptional – meaning they are the exception. Buffett is certainly someone to admire, study and model. However, your mind can also view what he has achieved as 'impossible' for you. It's all very well to talk about the benefits of compounding over 30, 40 or in Buffett's case nearly 80 years, but really, who invests for that sort of timeframe? Delayed returns, our money personalities and our mental biases make that timeframe feel like a lifetime – which it is.

It should also be noted that what Buffett has achieved in his career, business ventures and investment life is what he wanted to achieve. It is what he set out to do from age 14. It was his goal, and he has achieved it.

But it's very likely Buffett's goals are not your goals, so you shouldn't fall into the comparison trap. Study his thinking, his processes and his strategies – but separate what you want to achieve from his achievements, because you are different and will therefore have different priorities.

Time heals all

One of the biggest mistakes newly minted investors make is not understanding that time heals with compounding. They become afraid if they experience any loss, and don't give their investment time to grow.

A caveat to start: when we're talking about growth assets like shares and property, 'long term' is usually regarded as five-plus years. Seven-plus years is even better. Remember that as we go along.

Let me tell you the story of the unluckiest investor in Australia.

On 1 November 2007, an investor decided to buy into the S&P/ ASX 200. It looked like a great investment, having climbed 125 per cent over the previous four years – so after years of waiting the investor finally entered the market.

The very next day the market eased. No matter: the investor understood this could happen, and it was only one day. The market eased further over the next month and continued to do so. By the end of 2007 the investor's investment had lost 7.5 per cent.

What the investor didn't know at the time was they had brought the S&P/ASX 200 at its then-record all-time high – and that the Global Financial Crisis had begun.

It would take until 6 March 2009 for the market to stop falling. It reached its bottom some 15 months after the investor's initial investment. The value of the initial investment was now 54 per cent less than it was on 1 November 2007 (see figure 7.5).

Figure 7.5: The unluckiest investor 2007–2009

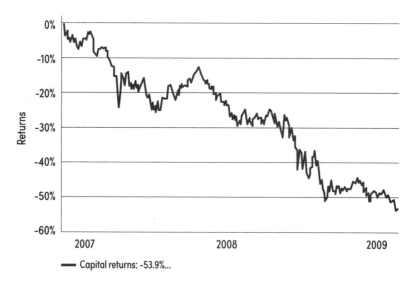

Capital returns: -53.9%...

Source: Refinitiv Datastream, InvestSMART

It would take another 12 years for the investor's capital to recover and break even – *12 years* (see figure 7.6).

Figure 7.6: The unluckiest investor 2007–2020

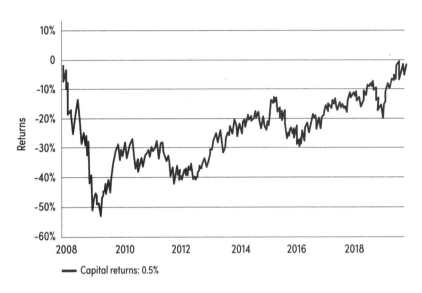

— Capital returns: 0.5%

Source: Refinitiv Datastream, InvestSMART

This would be enough to break any investor, even the very best: 12 years and no capital growth. This kind of situation is unfortunately what captures most people's attention, as biases like loss aversion, attention bias and anxiety hone in on the emotion involved in such a loss-making scenario.

This assumption, however, ignores the fundamental maths of compounding. The S&P/ASX 200 is the highest-dividend-paying developed market on the planet. And because the investor was receiving dividends during the 12 years and was reinvesting them to take advantage of compounding returns – which is referred to as total returns (capital and income combined) – the situation was not so dire (see figure 7.7).

Figure 7.7: The unluckiest investor – time heals all

Source: Refinitiv Datastream, InvestSMART

Once total returns are considered, the investor is no longer the unluckiest investor – just unlucky. They would have recouped their initial investment in mid-September 2013 and profited a further 72 per cent come 28 November 2019 – the same date the investor had waited to break even on a capital basis. This is why compound returns are so important, and why time does indeed heal all.

Even the unluckiest investor buying at the very top of the market will, over time, benefit from the beauty of compounding returns. This is just one example of an almost infinite list that's not limited to the Australian market – there are examples of this in every developed market on the planet.

There are several questions you need to ask yourself here: could you have absorbed the initial loss? Would your loss aversion bias have overridden your rational understanding that compound growth would eventually make up for the initial decline?

Again, even the most seasoned investor would have felt the hurt of these movements – you would not be alone in thinking negatively about your finances in this situation.

There are strategies and habits you can use to address this, which we will discuss in coming chapters. But for now, understand that time works in your favour when you invest.

Debt: when compounding *doesn't* work in your favour

Compounding over time may work in your favour when you invest, but it works against you when you borrow.

A home loan is a classic example of a long-term debt. Let's say you borrow $500,000 to buy a home, at an interest rate of 2.24 per cent (the average rate in early 2022), repayable over 25 years. If you stick to the lender's minimum repayments you will end up repaying a total of $668,400, including $168,400 in interest – 33 per cent of the amount you borrow.

The percentage is so high because, when it comes to debt, the power of compounding works to benefit the lender. The only way you can swing the pendulum in your favour is by paying off more than the minimum amount to weaken the impact of compounding.

As a guide, using the $500,000 loan example above, if you repay an extra $5 per day – about the price of a takeaway coffee – you can cut the total interest bill by $15,400.

The good thing about real estate is that the value of your home is likely to appreciate over that 25-year time period. Like any market, the housing market will have down periods; but over time it will appreciate, so the interest cost will have been worth it.

If you were to take on a personal loan or other debt scheme, the asset you purchase with this debt is likely to be a depreciating asset.

This means that not only have you added significantly to the purchase price by funding it with debt, but once you have finally paid off the debt the asset you purchased could very well have a value of zero – or near enough to. Before funding a depreciating purchase with debt, you should ask yourself: *will this be worth it?*

Compounding can work for you or against you. In the case of debt, you need to use it wisely. It can be a powerful tool, but a tool that can cause injury if used incorrectly.

Why some of us embrace time more than others

How do things like culture influence our willingness to embrace time? The traditional economic view that humans behave rationally doesn't allow for cultural differences – the individual or collective mindsets that differ across the cultures of the world. We now know this needs more investigation, since rationality is not the only way we make decisions.

A 2016 study looked at patience in investors from a selection of 53 different countries. In the study, participants were asked to select between receiving $3400 this month, or waiting and receiving $3800 next month. The Germanic/Nordic respondents were most likely to wait for a higher return in the future with 85 per cent surveyed choosing to wait, while those of African descent had the lowest percentage of participants choosing to wait with only 33 per cent.

Drilling down into the results by country of origin, the results show 51 per cent of Australians ticked the 'wait' option, making Australia the 12th most impatient nationality, with Germans ranking the most patient with 89 per cent of those surveyed prepared to wait. Nigerians are the least patient with less than 8 per cent prepared to wait. The study suggests that our personal biases around impatience, short-term gratification and value can be influenced by our culture. This could be a function of life experience, education, upbringing, socio-economic status and all the other factors that shape our views around money.

Culture is a major key to understanding your relationship with money. How you relate to and interact with family, extended family, neighbours, peers, colleagues and the like is not just down to your cognitive and emotional biases, but also to how your culture defines these relationships – and money has a big part to play here. That's what we will explore in the next chapter.

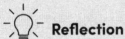 **Reflection**

- How does the concept of discounting relate to your own views and behaviours around money?
- What lessons can you take from the unluckiest investor story?
- Are you surprised by where Australians sit in terms of investment patience? If you're from a different culture, how can you use that information to glean a better understanding of your relationship with patience?

Chapter 8

Money culture

The beauty of the world lies in the diversity of its people.
– Unknown

One of the fastest-growing areas in behavioural finance is cultural finance. It is young, it is exciting and it is contested.

Traditional economic and financial thought says that all people around the world view their financial goals similarly. The conclusion is that there is a one-size-fits-all approach to dealing with people's long-term finances.

As soon as you read that statement, you will instinctively know it is wrong. You will know from your own culture that a one-size fit doesn't work in targeted culture, let alone the thousands of cultures all over the world.

We also know that culture has a huge influence on our views, beliefs and relationships, and when you think about those areas you will realise that your cultural money behaviour sits inside every one of them.

Let's consider some examples. Household saving rates in China are statistically higher relative to other countries. Under research conditions no real answer for this phenomenon has been found. However, when you view it through a cultural lens, there is a suggestion that the one-child policy meant households needed less money to bring up children but more for later in life as there would be fewer children to lean on during retirement. This could be what has incentivised household savings.

There is a cultural saying in Germany: *geld stinkt nicht* (cash doesn't sink). It is a well-known fact that Germans are high users of physical cash. Studies by the European Central Bank and others have found that Germans are more than twice as likely as their European neighbours to pay for everyday items with cash. Germans also have the lowest take-up of credit cards and personal debt in Europe. The cultural finance explanation for this behaviour is the historical collective memory of hyperinflation during the Weimar Republic era and the social unrest this caused.

In India, wealth and success is wrapped up in the ownership and symbolism of gold. Gold is at the very centre of many traditional rituals and present-giving events. As a result, India regularly has the highest demand for gold as an asset – either as a physical unit or as a paper contract (an ETF in physical gold). Only China can match India in its demand for and attraction to gold.

Defining culture

First, let me start by saying this: there really is no one way to define culture, and that is its beauty. Culture is diverse, free-flowing and ever-changing. It is traditional and progressive, inclusive and exclusive, domestic and international all at the same time.

However, many people have tried, so let's start with one of the founding thinkers of cultural psychology: Dutch sociologist Geert Hofstede.

Hofstede defined culture as 'a collective mental programming of the mind which is manifested in values and norms, but also in rituals and symbols'. This high-level definition is basically saying that we interact, make decisions and form behavioural biases from an array of social and cultural cues and norms.

Hofstede's studies led him to develop his six cultural dimensions. I am sure you will recognise most of these (illustrated in figure 8.1) as his work has become so renowned it has slipped into common thinking.

Figure 8.1: Hofstede's six cultural dimensions

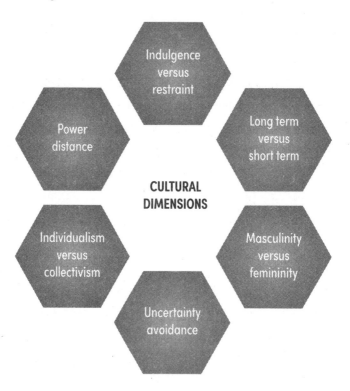

Source: Geert Hofstede 2011, 'Dimensionalizing Cultures: The Hofstede Model in Context', *Online Readings in Psychology and Culture*, vol. 2, no. 1.

For clarity here is how Hofstede defined each dimension:

- **Power distance**
  - *High:* Strong attachment to a hierarchical order in which everybody has a place and no further justification is needed.
  - *Low:* People endeavour to equalise the distribution of power. If this is lost they will demand justification for inequalities of power.

- **Indulgence versus restraint**
  - *Indulgence:* Allows relatively free gratification of basic and natural human drives – these being the enjoyment of life and having fun.
  - *Restraint:* Suppresses gratification of needs. Will regulate these needs by means of strict social norms.

- **Long-term orientation versus short-term orientation**
  - *Long term:* Pragmatic; encouragement of thrift. Sees modern education as a way to prepare for the future.
  - *Short term:* Looks to maintain time-honoured traditions and norms. Views societal change with suspicion.

- **Masculinity versus femininity**
  - *Masculinity:* Societal preference for the characteristics of achievement, heroism, assertiveness and material rewards for success.
  - *Femininity:* Societal preference for the characteristics of cooperation, modesty, caring for the weak and quality of life.

- **Uncertainty avoidance**
  - *High:* Society has rigid codes of beliefs and behaviours and a high level of intolerance for unorthodox behaviours and ideas.
  - *Low:* Society has a more accepting and relaxed attitude to behaviour and codes of conduct where practice counts more than principles.

- **Individualism versus collectivism**
  - *Individualism:* The preference for a loose social framework.
  - *Collectivism:* The preference for a tight-knit social framework.

The six dimensions sit on something of sliding scale between each opposing point. They are also interlinked and cross over. So, for example, individualism, tolerance of uncertainty and masculinity are linked in their ideas, and the same can be said about femininity, collectivism and restraint.

Over the years, this dimension framework has been used to group societies on a geographical basis – for example, defining a collectivist society as typical of East Asia, where an individual's identity is considered as part of a larger social group. This contrasts with an individualistic society, such as Western Europe, Australia or the US, where personal values and achievements are more important than those of the larger social group.

However, this wide grouping is way too simplistic. Certain European cultures would be more aligned with collectivism than individualism, and there are parts of Asia that are more individualistic than collective.

Again, this shows why money culture as a concept is contentious, but it does raise some fascinating money behaviour trends that need to be explored. To do this, let's dive back into a behavioural bias we've already discussed – loss aversion. But this time, let's consider loss aversion alongside the dimension of culture.

Loss aversion

In a 2010 study, German behavioural finance experts Dr Thorsten Hens, Dr Mei Wang and Dr Marc Oliver Rieger examined the risk and behavioural biases of nearly 7000 investors in 53 countries. They found that the cultural dimensions of individualism, power distance and masculinity are significantly correlated with loss aversion.

This makes sense, as individualist cultures affiliate more with ideas of self-enhancement and independence. That is, people (investors) value and care more about an object (their investment) that is associated with themselves, and a loss of the object (the investment) is seen as a reflection on them.

Contrast this with those from collectivist cultures who tend to adopt holistic perspectives of a single object (their investment) and are therefore more able to cope with losses. The 'collective society' is also more likely to support the individual from a loss, which makes these investors less sensitive to losses.

I find this idea really interesting, as it goes to the very heart of money culture. For example, look at how Mediterranean cultures use money inside the 'family'. And by family, I mean the full extended 'cousins of cousins' family. The pool of money in the family is used to help all inside this community.

Need a deposit for a house? The family will provide the deposit. Need to renovate said house? The family works together providing the trades and services each member has, keeping costs low and returns for the family high. Want to start a business? The family will provide the financial backing required.

This is not limited to Mediterranean cultures, either: Arabic and Asian cultures work in similar ways.

Another version of this idea comes from Latin America and the Caribbean. It's known as 'Tanda'– a kind of co-op banking system inside a defined community.

Simply put, it works a little like this: a group of people (the extended family, the village, the community) each save an agreed amount that is added to a collective pool on a specified day – this tends to be payday, or the first day of the calendar month. The collective pool then uses a rotating turn system to pay out the fund. On turn one, one member of the collective receives a payout; on turn two, the next member receives a payout; and so on until all members of the collective have had a turn. No interest is created, but it's a saving pool from which everyone knows they will be able to draw.

There are other countries and regions with similar concepts to Tanda – South Africa, for example, has Stokvels. It shows how a collective culture can positively impact everyone's relationship with money.

Contrast this with Western cultures, which work around the nuclear family and have only had to go to the bank of Mum and Dad in the past few decades. The concept of sharing wealth across the extended family is foreign for individualism.

This comes back to the impact loss aversion has on individual cultures – the pool of funds is smaller as it's just the nuclear family, and therefore loss is felt more strongly as the impact on the family's financial wellbeing is higher.

Power distance

Let's dive into another cultural dimension – this time, power distance. Hofstede measured power distance as an index from 0 to 100. The higher the power distance, the more rigid the society is to hierarchy and the more it discourages assertiveness and emotion.

Looking at this from the context of cultural finance, if inequality is high (that is, it has a high power distance), the average individual is more likely to feel helpless about loss. Therefore, the higher the power distance in a culture, the higher the level of loss aversion people in that culture might have.

Figure 8.2 shows the differences in investor loss aversion based on power distance.

What the chart shows is that people from countries with high degrees of hierarchical order are more likely to exhibit issues with loss and be more affected by a loss of cash and wealth.

Figure 8.2: International differences in investor loss aversion based on power distance

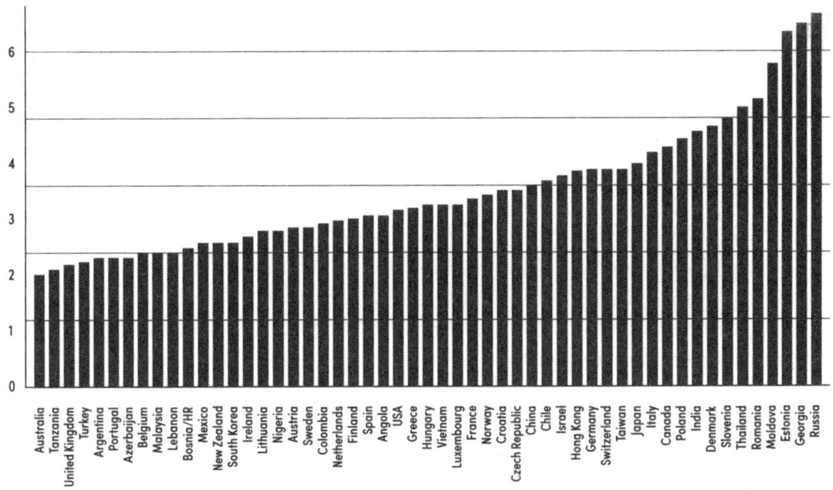

Source: Dr Thorsten Hens & Anna Meier 2016, 'Behavioral finance: The psychology of investing', CreditSuisse, credit-suisse.com/media/assets/private-banking/docs/mx/wp-07-behavioral-finance-en.pdf.

Where culture gets really interesting is the behaviour taken once a loss occurs. In chapter 3, I described a study by Kahneman and Tversky that found people would take a guaranteed $900, rather than taking a 90 per cent chance of gaining $1000 with a 10 per cent risk of losing it all. The Hens, Wang and Rieger study referenced earlier in this chapter found that *all* cultures have a high inclination to risk more after losing money. In other words, there is no statistical difference between cultures about what to do to 'get even', as every culture surveyed would take the risk and try to recoup losses with even more risk-taking. The researchers coined this 'get-even-itis'.

Here is the country outcome for 'get-even-itis' – that is, the inclination to risk even more money to avoid a definite loss.

Figure 8.3: International differences in the inclination to risk more money to avoid a definite loss

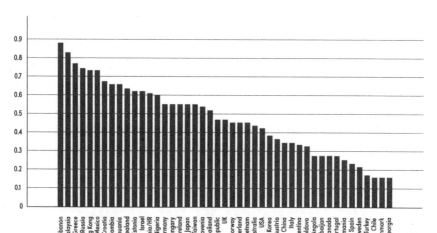

Source: Dr Thorsten Hens & Anna Meier 2016, 'Behavioral finance: The psychology of investing', CreditSuisse, c
redit-suisse.com/media/assets/private-banking/docs/mx/wp-07-behavioral-finance-en.pdf.

There is a universal link in investor behaviour around loss: if we can avoid loss altogether, we are willing to take on higher risk to achieve this. It is an unfortunate trait, as chasing your losses is more likely to end with even higher losses. It's something we all need to be aware of, as it is a behavioural and cultural bias for all.

Uncertainty avoidance

Another interesting cultural dimension to delve into more deeply is uncertainty avoidance (UA). This is the measure of a society's tolerance for uncertainty and ambiguity.

UA impacts people's views on time. Why? Those cultures that have a higher UA score tend to be less tolerant of uncertain situations. As the future is unpredictable, high UA cultures tend to prefer immediate rewards rather than future rewards.

What that means from a money viewpoint is that high UA cultures prefer investment options like dividends or deposit yields, rather than waiting for future rewards like total returns. And as we know, the advantages of investing and diversifying your money over time is likely to help you achieve greater financial freedom. For example, this could explain why Japanese investors are more likely to invest in bonds and fixed income securities, as they have a high UA rating compared to US investors, who are more likely to invest in higher-risk securities as they have a low UA rating.

Your own cultural money upbringing

Of course, as well as the wider culture of the country we live in, the culture within our individual families also impacts our money identity and behaviour.

Every family culture is different, and inside that culture you will find that money is discussed, used and saved in a multitude of ways.

I am going to use the story of my mum's investment journey to explain this further.

Money was never discussed in the Lucas household while I was growing up – like, *never*! I knew my parents had some money, but what they did with it – how they used and spent it – was never discussed. Period.

As a kid that was fine – until my father lost his job, lost his brother to heart disease and had a breakdown. This saw him land in a clinic for more than three months. At the time I was 16 and my sister was 12 going on 13, and we couldn't fully comprehend the scale of change that was taking place. Money became tight and spending slowed, however my parents continued almost as if nothing had really changed. They made it their mission that their change of circumstance would not affect my sister or me.

Through this whole period money was still not discussed; it was not in our family culture to burden the children with money stress. This is completely understandable, but of course it still did affect us. That event changed my relationship with money. It probably explains why in my younger years I didn't go into debt, why I only used what I had and why saving was something important to me.

What is so strange about my parents' situation is that the culture my mum grew up in was essentially the same: money wasn't discussed – ever. Living frugally, working hard for what you had and enjoying what you made was their culture. What was different, however, was my grandfather's ability with money.

Mum's father – who I spoke of briefly in chapter 2 – was an amazing retail share investor. He bought Rio Tinto and BHP in the 1970s; he bought both CBA and CSL in their 1994 initial public offerings (IPOs); he also bought Telstra in all three IPO tranches throughout the 1990s. He loved his Woolworths and Wesfarmers shares so much he would buy parcels of them every year without fail.

He had sovereign fixed income by buying ETFs, hybrids and a tonne of corporate bonds, and to cap it all off, he held a minimum of two term deposits (TDs) at all times so that even his cash was working for him. He saw TDs as his today money; everything else was for tomorrow and beyond.

By the time he passed away, on the penultimate day of 2017, he had over 25 holdings in some of Australia's most trusted companies and a few up-and-comers too. He was well diversified with all asset classes covered and was basically earning a good wage from his investment portfolio at the end. He was 93 when he passed, and we called him Grampie.

The key takeaways from Grampie's money journey are:

- He invested for the long term.
- He reinvested all earnings for most of his working life, before drawing on the income later in life.
- He participated in anything that he believed would grow his capital.
- Every piece of cash was 'working' – it was invested in something to gain a return.

Needless to say, Grampie's portfolio was legendary in the family. When I first became aware of Grampie's investment habits I was fascinated. I loved watching him study his portfolio and read the business section of the newspaper with yesterday's individual stock prices so he knew where his portfolio stood. We would talk about all this for hours and he would show me how he did what he did, and why. The learning from these chats was steep, and better than any degree I have earned.

As I got older and took up investing as my vocation, Grampie would ring me for 'investment advice'.

I would respond with: 'I think you have that the wrong way around – *I* need advice from *you*.'

I do miss him, and as I sit here and write about this, I remember why I love what I do, why I do it and why I got into it. I was lucky enough to be in a cultural environment that helped me find financial freedom.

I find it interesting that none of Grampie's four children took up that culture. Maybe it was because they didn't discuss money or personal finance. Maybe it was against their own nuclear family culture to consider something like investing as a topic of discussion. I will never know. But I will say this: Grampie never pushed his kids to invest, which I think was a mistake.

This is why it fell to me to get the ball rolling with Mum. I had been pushing Mum to invest since I can remember – before even entering this field of work.

She had plenty of excuses: 'Oh, I don't know how' (yes, I was telling her that I would help); 'I don't have the time'; 'I don't have enough money'; 'I can't afford to lose my money's value'.

Each excuse would be accompanied by a statement like: 'I wish I had started when Dad did' or 'I suggested to your father that we should have done this years ago'. My comment in reply was always, 'So, why didn't you?' And we would then loop back to 'I don't know how' and 'I don't have the time'.

I could sense some underlying hesitation in Mum. It was not in her culture to talk about money, wealth or investing, and this I believe is something that added to her resistance to start her investing journey.

Then COVID-19 hit and, as it did most of us, it impacted her working life and source of income. The 'great reset' that was COVID-19 finally forced her to confront her bias and money personality and led her to realise she needed to do something different. Then came her message to me: 'Help me get started. I can't afford to put this off anymore' – verbatim.

Now, I won't divulge Mum's age or other personal demographics, but I will say this: she is at an age where she would like her money to be growing, but she knows she will want to start drawing on it in the near future (within five to 10 years). She can contribute $500 a month to her initial investment to compound her returns. And she wants the process and the investment to be easy, as she doesn't have the time like Grampie did to pore over the papers and work out which stocks or markets to invest in.

This led to her decision to invest in simple index-linked ETFs across all asset classes weighted towards a growth profile with a simple contribution plan attached.

She couldn't be happier. She said the process was easy and now that she has actually started, she can't believe she put up so many roadblocks. In fact, she believes she has more 'peace of mind' now that it's up and running than before when she was deliberating about what to do and kept putting it off.

Mum: 'Wish you had pushed me into this sooner.'

Me: 'Mum, I have been at you about this for more than 17 years.'

What Mum's decision shows is that it's never too late to start. I know Grampie would be happy to know Mum has started investing after all these years too. But my biggest insight is that our family's culture was a clear obstacle, and that behavioural bias led to Mum waiting a lot longer than she needed to.

This is why culture is so important for your own money and financial freedom. What we've discussed here is only the tip of the massive iceberg that is cultural finance. It's a space that will be investigated more and more in the coming years. There are so many questions yet to be answered. For example, does globalisation and the integration of people across geographic areas reset some cultural money habits, or do people tend to retain the culture from where they were born? Can cultures embrace the more helpful money behaviours that so-called opposing cultures exhibit? Time will tell.

From your own personal money perspective, embracing different cultural ideas around money could accelerate your quest for financial freedom.

To be clear, money should not define you, and it is unfortunate that in some parts of society and culture it does. This shallowness is linked to all manner of issues, but there is no escaping that is it also a very deeply ingrained social norm in most cultures. The collision of money and behaviour, of judgement and stigma, is something we should all wish to change. The question that raises is: who do you start with, society or yourself? I would like to say 'society', but that may not be in our individual control. It's easier to start from the individual level – to be the change you want to see in the world. Group ignorance is a very powerful force. At the individual level you have the power to control your destiny; and the help that is available is more likely to be tailored to an individual level rather than a societal level. This is far from the best outcome, but if a sole individual can improve their financial situation even modestly and can then pass that learning on to the next generation, the change we need to see around the use of money will spread.

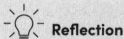 **Reflection**

· Can you identify money hurdles and constraints in your own culture? How does your culture view loss, power and uncertainty?
· What traits in other cultures might be beneficial to you and your social group?
· Does your family culture help or hinder your relationship, openness and adaptability with money and investing?

Chapter 9

Loving the scary ugly

Fear has a far greater grasp on human action than the
impressive weight of historical evidence.
– Jeremy Siegel

We all love a beautiful thing. 'A thing of beauty is a joy forever' said 19th century English poet John Keats. But it's not just the romantic poet's opinion. Steve Jobs placed 'simplicity and beauty' at the core of Apple's product design, and scientists have proven that it is natural for humans to be drawn to the beautiful rather than the scary and ugly.

Over the past decade multiple brain scan studies have discovered the remarkable fact that the mere sight of an attractive product can trigger the motor cortex, the part of the brain that controls hand movement. In other words, we instinctively reach for attractive things.

This is not a modern phenomenon; humans have displayed this behaviour for millennia. Ancient philosophers described the golden rectangle, a phenomenon that has been marvelled at by mathematicians and artists over the ages. A golden rectangle is a rectangle with side lengths in a particular ratio – the 'golden ratio'. Subtract a square from a golden rectangle, and what remains is another golden rectangle. Do it again, and there's a new golden rectangle – it's an infinite spiral (see figure 9.1).

Figure 9.1: The golden rectangle

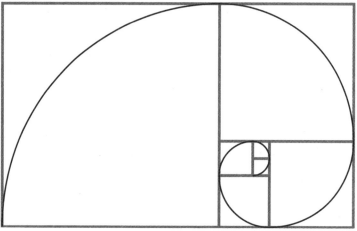

Figure 9.2 shows the mathematics of the golden rectangle. Once you look at this image you will be able to recognise it in common in everyday things: think of the shape of your television, laptop screen, credit card and bank notes (although you don't see too many of those around these days). Yes, your cash is aesthetically pleasing on a subconscious level. Even this book is a golden rectangle.

Figure 9.2: The mathematics of the golden rectangle

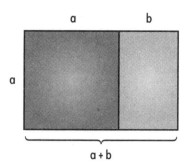

Golden rectangles have been used in structures from the Pyramids of Giza to the Parthenon, Notre-Dame and Taj Mahal. Golden rectangles can be seen in the face of Mona Lisa and in Michelangelo's 'Creation of Adam', where two are seen side-by-side.

The takeout is that our mind instinctively gravitates to things that are aesthetically pleasing.

Fearing the ugly

Conversely, studies have proven that we fear the ugly. When we see attractive things, this lights up our motor cortex and sees us instinctively reach for them, whereas fear lights up another part of the brain: the amygdala. The amygdala's main job is to trigger your nervous system, which in turn sets off your body's fear response with hormone releases. Cortisol and adrenaline start to run riot causing higher blood pressure, higher heart rate and faster breathing.

What's more, the flow of blood in your body changes direction by moving away from your vital organs, such as your heart and liver, and towards your legs and arms – because you might have to start throwing haymakers or turn into Usain Bolt and... bolt.

The thing about fear is that everyone has a slightly different reaction to it. For some, fear is something to thrive on. Bungee jumpers, free climbers, horror movie fans – these people get a buzz from fear! For others there is nothing worse than being spooked; fear is a horrible experience from start to finish. This reaction leads to high levels of avoidance.

What is so interesting about fear is that part of the body's response is to release dopamine – known as the pleasure hormone. According to physiologists this could explain why some get a kick out of fear and others don't. Until recently we didn't fully understand that dopamine also assists us in avoiding pain and fear from negative stimulation.

Whichever category you fall into, the physiological reason to fear is designed to keep you safe; it is a natural biological function.

However, from a psychological viewpoint, fear can be a problem if you don't harness it in the correct fashion. As I mentioned earlier, fear causes a physical response, as your body is powered to move to survive. With the blood supply diverted to the parts of the body responsible for physical escape, there is less available to the brain – specifically the cerebral cortex, which is responsible for high-level things like reasoning and judgement. That lower blood supply makes it difficult for us to make reasoned decisions or to think clearly when we're afraid. This explains why you might scream uncontrollably at a horror movie or put your hands up to protect yourself when your partner jumps out and yells 'Boo'. Both times you have been unable to rationalise that neither situation is a real threat.

There are very few people in the world who are able to combine fear and attraction on a physiological basis. One of them is rock climber Alex Honnold, who managed to free climb (without ropes or safety mechanisms) El Capitan in Yosemite National Park. The face of El Capitan is 975 metres straight up. Honnold describes El Capitan as the most impressive wall on Earth. His skill, coupled with his strength of mind, allowed him to conquer his fear and attraction in equal measure. He became the first person in history to free climb El Capitan. He epitomises how your mind is key to your output.

To deal with the competing functions of fear and attraction we need to harness our mind's ability to control our emotions. This is easier said than done, as again our reactions to fear are infinite and varied. There is no one-size-fits-all technique to harness our emotions.

Now that we understand better how fear and attraction affect our physical and emotional responses, let's a take a look at how they play out in the worlds of investing and money management.

Turning an ugly duckling into a swan

Investing is often presented as an ugly duckling situation. What I mean by this is that daily, weekly and monthly movements in investment markets can look and feel 'ugly'. Remember the fairy-tale, though? The ugly duckling eventually grows into a beautiful swan. Let's have a look at this transformation.

One of the ways to make investment costs and returns more attractive is to calculate the average – rather than focus on the short-term fluctuations. Consider some common statistics from the world of money:

· Interest repayments are 2.5 per cent per annum of the amount you have borrowed.
· The return on your savings account is 1.05 per cent per annum.
· The average return of your investment portfolio is 9.8 per cent per annum.

If we turn some of these examples in chart form (figure 9.3) we can see how pleasing they are to the eye.

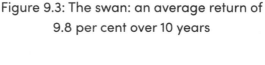

Figure 9.3: The swan: an average return of 9.8 per cent over 10 years

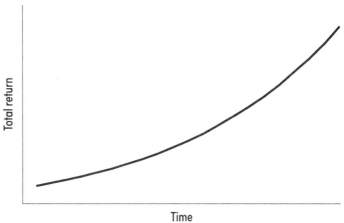

There's a very good-looking upward growth trajectory, powered in large part by compounding (which we discussed in chapter 7).

I chose 9.8 per cent because this is the actual average annual return of the S&P/ASX 200 over the past 10 years. This is how your holding would have grown over the past 10 years on average, if you had invested in this index and reinvested your returns. The total return on your initial investment would be a staggering 157 per cent!

The question you may ask is, in which year did the S&P/ASX 200 actually return exactly 9.8 per cent? You might be surprised to learn that the answer is 'in no year'. Not once in the past 10 years would the market actually have given you its average. The closest year to the average was 2016 when the S&P/ASX 200 gave a total return of 11.8 per cent.

Moving on from the attractive graph above, let's consider fear and the ugly. Figure 9.4 charts the same investment (the S&P/ASX 200) over the same period, but there is more detail – the short-term price movements are graphed.

Figure 9.4: The ugly duckling

Source: Refinitiv Datastream, InvestSMART

Again, this is the actual performance of the S&P/ASX 200 over the same 10-year period. There are no golden rectangles in this chart, and for many investors it will cause their amygdala to run its finger over the panic button. Just look at the sharp declines in some of those years. There have been some ugly periods over the past decade, due in large part to unforeseen global events:

- The European debt crisis in 2012
- The US taper tantrum in 2013
- China's hard landing in 2015/16
- The US rate rise correction in 2018
- The outbreak of the global COVID-19 pandemic in 2020.

Yet, despite all of these horrific world events, the y-axis tells us that the index has returned a total of 157 per cent.

Watching the ugly scenario of your investments losing money plays out in two ways. First, it causes your loss aversion bias to kick in, making you question your decision-making and lowering your resolve. Second, it elicits a physiological fear response – and this happens to everyone.

I would bet that there is not one person in the history of investing who has not experienced that fear of loss. The difference between those who handle this fear well and those who don't is how they react to the fear. What processes do they have in place to mitigate losses?

Let me tell you about a very close colleague's initial reaction to the COVID-19 outbreak in March 2020. On 9 March, I got a call from someone in financial markets whom I really admire. I answered the phone in an artificially cheery tone in an effort to counter the unforeseen misery that was taking hold around the globe. This is what this person said to me:

'Evan, I want to liquidate everything in my superannuation scheme and go to cash. I think this is "the one". This is the event that brings everything down. What do you think will be the easiest way to do that?'

Floored, I blurted out: 'Why would you want to do that?'

His response: 'The risk is just too great to wait. We are never coming back from this.'

He was in his mid to late 30s at the time, meaning he would have to almost double his age before he could access this money under Australia's superannuation laws. In other words, he would have to live a second lifetime before touching this pool of funds.

This person has worked in financial markets for nearly two decades and has seen all manner of events that have caused issues like the pandemic did. But, in a moment of fear, staring at a particularly ugly trading day (the market lost 7.32 per cent on March 9), he lost control.

I had to reassure him. 'You definitely don't want to do that,' I responded. 'The health crisis will end sometime in the future; markets will digest the fallout and reprice the risk; people will learn, grow and prosper into the future. Your super will gain from this and in 30 years' time COVID will look like another short blip event in your investment journey.'

His response: 'Ignore me – moment of weakness.' It may have been, but for a few minutes he had actually considered this drastic action.

My colleague later moved in to more assertive holdings. He bought low and took full advantage of the recovery in mid-2020 and through 2021. And he reminds me constantly of how crushing it would have been had he liquidated all his shares and gone to cash.

There is no doubt that this was a fear response. Everything in my colleague's vision about the state of affairs was creating a flight response to protect his nest egg.

This should also give you solace that even the very best can be affected by the psychological and physiological fear response caused by big loss-making events. The question you need to ask is whether in a moment of weakness you would have panicked too!

It's a matter of perspective

This where you need to reorientate your viewpoint. You need to pivot away from the factors that play against you – short-termism, losses in individual markets or holdings and doomscrolling through endless negativity, which leads you to think that your investments might be wrong. You have to adopt a wider perspective, look at a longer timeframe, stand back to take in the bigger picture and remove negative inputs that impact your behaviour towards money.

Here are some critical statistics around the US S&P 500 index that will give you greater perspective and help to allay your fears.

Over the last 122 years, the S&P 500 has averaged one correction a year. (A correction is regarded as a decline of 10 per cent or more.) That doesn't mean there's been a correction every year; you might have seen two or more declines in one year and none in another. The perspective you are getting here is that market declines are normal and to be expected.

The average length of each of these corrections was 54 days – less than two months. Remember, most economic data and financial earnings are reported every quarter. By the time you receive the report on the correction, it could well have corrected itself (excuse the pun). Having a reaction to a 54-day event is not taking a long-term view. You have not given yourself enough time-based evidence to make a clear decision; rather, you have panicked.

The average loss across these corrections was 13.5 per cent. This will look and feel like a lot, particularly for those of you who have strong loss aversion biases – you might see this as possibly too much to bear.

Let's widen our perspective and look at a different asset class – property. If you had a massive neon sign attached to the top of your house telling you its exact value for six hours of every day, and one day you saw that the value of your home had fallen 13.5 per cent, would you sell it? I doubt it. You need to apply the same logic to your other assets.

If we switch markets and this time use the S&P/ASX 200 as the baseline, we can see similar trends.

Over the past 30 years, the S&P/ASX 200 has experienced 20 corrections, of which only four have turned into bear markets (a bear market is where a market falls 20 per cent or more). Three of the four have been due to crises, such as the Asian financial crisis, the Global Financial Crisis and the COVID-19 pandemic.

The average correction lasted approximately 48 days. Again, less than two months.

The S&P/ASX 200 also has an interesting difference to its global peers in developed markets. It has been the highest-yielding index according to the MSCI, averaging 4.25 per cent per annum. That makes it a very interesting market for compound returns. Take a look at figure 9.5.

Figure 9.5: S&P/ASX 200 corrections and bears

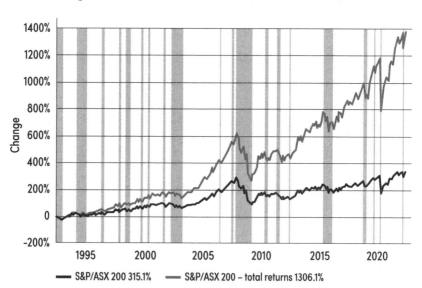

Source: Refinitiv Datastream, InvestSMART

Since 1992 the capital growth of the S&P/ASX 200 has been over 315 per cent. On a total return basis, where all returns are reinvested, the index has returned over 1300 per cent in the same time period.

All markets experience periods of volatility, triggering fear. All markets will lose ground at certain points during their lifetime. This is something we know, and it is not a new concept.

This is why looking at the S&P 500 or the S&P/ASX 200 in time isolation is setting yourself up for failure. Your mind will see the short-term losses from corrections and bear markets as highly detrimental, which can lead you to make adverse investment decisions.

Remember the ugly duckling? There's a beautiful swan behind that ugly chart.

Smoothing out the fear

So, thinking back to aesthetics, how can we smooth out the individual ugliness into something more palatable? We know volatility is part of the investment cycle – how can we learn to accept it despite it being ugly and scary?

We are all familiar with the saying 'Don't put all your eggs in one basket'. I secretly like to think this saying was coined by an investor, as it fits the concept of diversification almost too perfectly. Diversification is the way to smooth out the fear.

When looking at diversification, you must first define what assets are considered 'the same'. Are you diversifying the fundamentals of your equity holdings – for example, selecting bank stocks and resource stocks, or technology stocks and healthcare stocks, to have exposure over multiple sectors? Or is it broader than this? Are you seeking to spread your investments across different asset classes – think property, equities, cash, fixed income, alternative investments, digital assets (crypto) and metals?

In my experience, the more broadly you diversify, the more likely you are to smooth out volatility and improve your overall returns. You will also reduce the risk of making poor investment or bad money decisions.

The absolute authority in the power of asset diversification is Nobel Prize winning American economist Harry Markowitz. In 1952 Markowitz released his best-known work on the concept of modern portfolio theory. Modern portfolio theory stresses that an individual security should not be evaluated alone, and that its individual performance is actually not as important as the whole investment portfolio. It's a method that involves constructing a diversified portfolio that maximises returns inside a risk profile that is acceptable to the individual investor.

Markowitz showed that most investments are either high risk with high returns or low risk with low returns (see figure 9.6).

Figure 9.6: Risk-return trade-off

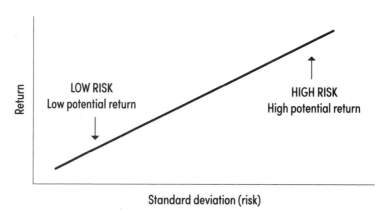

Standard deviation (risk)

To help explain risk versus reward and how we all view risk differently, let's return to rock climber Alex Honnold. He said of risk: 'I differentiate between risk and consequence. Sure, falling from this building is a high consequence, but, for me, it's low risk.'

What he is essentially saying is that the risk for him is not the same as it is for you or me. For us, free climbing has a high risk of death. For him, it's low risk, as there is a very low probability of a negative outcome due to his skill.

Markowitz argued that a blend of assets that suited the individual's risk tolerance was the best way to achieve their optimal return. The beauty of modern portfolio theory, from a behavioural finance viewpoint, is that it takes into account that what is best for you is not necessarily best for the next investor – and that your optimal return may be more or less than theirs.

Figure 9.7 tracks the performance over a five-year period of the individual asset classes that are considered vital to any diversified investment portfolio: domestic equities, international equities, domestic bonds, international bonds, property and cash.

Figure 9.7: Five-year performance of six asset classes

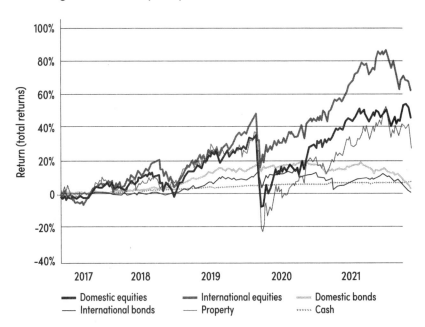

Source: Refinitiv Datastream, InvestSMART

If you had taken Markowitz's modern portfolio theory and constructed a 'balanced' portfolio, this is the performance you would have achieved over the past five years. A balanced portfolio comprises approximately 50 per cent defensive assets, such as fixed income and cash, and 50 per cent growth assets, such as domestic and international equities and property.

Using the S&P/ASX 200 as a baseline, figure 9.8 shows how much smoother and more consistent returns have been when the six asset classes are combined. Diversification doesn't completely safeguard against declines, but it does offer a buffer to their severity.

Figure 9.8: Balanced funds versus S&P/ASX 200

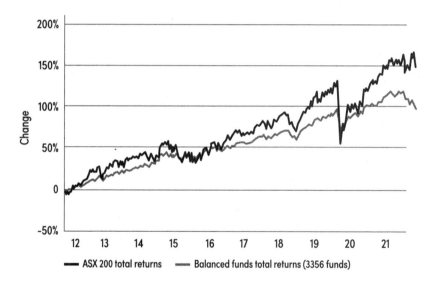

Source: Refinitiv Datastream, InvestSMART

Note that the balanced portfolio's performance is less than the S&P/ASX 200. This is expected, as the risk of the S&P/ASX 200 is higher than that of a balanced portfolio.

This highlights another challenge you'll need to address if you want to smooth out volatility: the fear of missing out (FOMO).

You might be thinking, 'I should have invested only in the equity market' or 'I shouldn't have missed out on that performance'. Time to get your mind over money here! Remember, you were after a low-risk investment approach because you could not tolerate the increased volatility displayed in an individual asset class. Focus on the positive: you're in a much better place to avoid panic that could lead to poor investment decisions.

Modern portfolio theory isn't perfect, but it can certainly minimise decision-making mistakes. Yet most investors miss out on the advantages of diversification. Why so?

The most likely reason is additional psychological bias. We discussed several biases earlier in the book, but there are two more to consider in relation to diversification: the ringfencing effect and familiarity bias.

Ringfencing

Ringfencing is the tendency to become hyper focused on specific investments or investment classes in your portfolio, rather than considering the wider view of your portfolio overall. This bias is particularly strong when that investment or asset class confirms your self-attribution bias, which we discussed in chapter 3.

Having a narrow focus 'borders' your thinking and 'ringfences' each investment inside the portfolio. The issue with ringfencing is that you treat each asset class separately rather than thinking of it as part of a whole, and this diminishes the power of diversification. The hypersensitivities caused by loss aversion and confirmation bias lead you back to the mistakes of bad decision-making, and Markowitz's optimal returns from diversification are lost.

One of the best ways to counter the effect of ringfencing is to simplify your investment holdings. Having too many investments, or adding investments to your portfolio that are outside of your stated investment strategy, will encourage the ringfencing approach. You overcome ringfencing by adopting a wider focus – by looking at a security or asset class as a percentage of the whole portfolio rather than seeing it as an individual performer.

Familiarity bias

Familiarity bias is the second inhibitor of diversification. As humans, we naturally gravitate towards the familiar. In social settings, we are drawn to familiar groups as we know the rules and can easily fit into the group's constructs. Think about when you go to a party: you naturally approach someone there who you know, rather than starting a conversation with a total stranger.

In behavioural finance, the same thing happens. Investors are more likely to invest in familiar investment classes and securities rather than look at unknown stocks or securities, even if they would offer better diversification.

Studies have shown that investors tend to invest in their own region, state, country or even their own industry of work, as these are all familiar investment environments.

Familiarity bias manifests most in the property market, where investors are inclined to buy an investment property in their home suburb – just because they like living there! Better-informed property investors make decisions based on regional growth drivers, rental returns and what tenants are seeking in a location – and building a diversified portfolio – rather than buying property just up the road because it's familiar to them.

Such decisions to invest locally are contrary to Markowitz's stated aims of diversification. Familiarity bias beds us to a 'home' bias, which can lead to over-allocating to the familiar rather than to the investments that offer the best returns in terms of their overall portfolio performance.

This point is particularly acute when comparing domestic and international equity investment. The recent annual ASX survey of Australian retail investors and their investment habits showed that only 27 per cent of those surveyed have some international equities, up from 17 per cent in 2014. Just over one in four investors holds international equities, despite international equities consistently outperforming Australian domestic equities over the past decade.

Worse still, the survey also showed that of those who held international equities, their allocation as a percentage of their overall portfolio was only 2 per cent. Once again, this highlights that their fund allocation is skewed to the familiar domestic assets, which have produced suboptimal performance over the past decade.

As with ringfencing, by reorientating your viewpoint you can overcome familiarity bias. If you only hold 2 per cent in international equities, what have you allocated the remaining 98 per cent to? Does it have a high domestic focus? If so, why? Probably because of your familiarity bias. Did it catch your attention, or was it because all the available information you had led you to the familiar option rather than the optimal option?

Asking these questions forces you to be honest with yourself. If you can't be honest with yourself, who can you be honest with? My advice: develop some investment discipline and reorientate your mind back to your money as a whole, which is the aim of the game in the end.

In the next chapter we'll explore this idea further – looking at the whole.

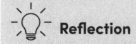 **Reflection**

- What is your relationship with fear? Are you a natural risk-taker or more conservative?
- What is your natural reaction to seeing a dip in your investment performance?
- Can you identify instances of ringfencing and familiarity bias in your own portfolio? What percentage of your portfolio is international?

Chapter 10

The elephant paradigm

*The only people who see the whole picture are the
ones who step out of the frame.*
– Salman Rushdie

One of my favourite analogies for understanding money is what I like
to call the elephant paradigm. It's based off a children's fable: how do
you eat an elephant? The answer is: one bite at a time.

The elephant paradigm infers many things, including that we
should break tasks, situations and life itself into more manageable
pieces so it won't overwhelm us. It is also an analogy for how psychology believes we process information. One of the things we do very
well as humans is break things down into small bite sizes.

The thing is, when it comes to your money that's not necessarily
the way you should look at it. You should work the elephant paradigm
in reverse. You need to be able to see the whole elephant, rather than
the small piece that is currently sitting on your plate.

Looking at the whole elephant can change your perception of
your overall wealth and the financial freedom that comes with what
you have.

Unfortunately, our default approach can be to home in on our personal savings, or the balance of our everyday account. Sometimes (though I suspect not very often) we may even check to see how much superannuation or retirement savings we've managed to accumulate.

We also have a tendency to look at our wealth through the lens of the physical objects we have (a car, a house, a boat) or what we have achieved (kids in a private school, annual vacations).

This tendency to look at bits and pieces of our wealth, rather than seeing the complete picture, leads to misconceptions about where we are financially.

If you picture an elephant in its entirety, notice that the trunk is perfectly proportioned to reach tall trees, the feet are suitably large to support the animal's great bulk, and those flapping ears are just right for cooling the body on hot days. While I admit the stumpy tail is questionable, the fact is if we view the elephant as a whole, it becomes clear that all the different body parts come together to work efficiently as a well-functioning animal.

It's the same with your finances. Having a holistic view of your wealth matters. It's not just about knowing how much you owe on your credit card this month, or when the car registration is due for payment. It's about being able to see the bigger picture of your true wealth. And frankly, if more of us were able to take a 360-degree view of our finances, we might feel more in control. Some would feel a sense of relief about their personal situation and some might realise they are actually reasonably well off.

It's very easy to fall into the habit of checking a banking app several times a day to see how your transaction account is tracking, or to sit down with a budgeting spreadsheet every so often to finetune spending. Don't get me wrong: these checks are all worthwhile. But you need to supplement this piecemeal approach with an overarching view of where you sit financially.

Rather than drowning you in detail, a big-picture perspective gives you a clear sense of where you stand now. Importantly, it also establishes a foundation to build on.

Seeing the whole elephant lets you appreciate what you have

When we see the big picture, many of us realise our finances don't look too bad after all. This can lead to us making firm plans to boost wealth rather than pinning our hopes on unrealistic wishes.

Many of us believe we need to earn a far higher salary just to feel rich. Anecdotal surveys have shown that one in four people wouldn't consider themselves affluent unless they were earning at least $500,000. In a 2022 survey, Australians said they would need to earn an annual salary of more than $325,000 – which is nearly seven times the (then) median personal income of $49,805 – to feel wealthy.

Constant longing for more money can be a dangerous game. Only a small percentage of high-income earners achieve those sorts of incomes. The reality is that the typical middle-class Australian is actually earning about $92,000 annually, according to the Australian Bureau of Statistics (ABS).

Add in the impact of social media, which can make it seem like everyone around you is hustling their way to the top, and it's easy to lose your perspective and feel like you are struggling. That's not the case for many Australians, and this becomes clearer when we look at the big picture.

The ABS crunched the data back in late 2020 and found the average Australian household had amassed net (after-debt) wealth of $1.02 million. We'll come back to this shortly, but given the growth in property values through to the start of 2022, it's fair to say homeowners would now be worth considerably more.

Seeing the whole elephant drives better choices

For many people, the default approach is to look at bits and pieces of their finances – chiefly those that impact us daily, like our everyday account balance, or maybe a share-trading account if events on the stock market are making headlines.

We tend to revisit other important numbers such as our super fund or home loan balance far less frequently – often only when the thought occurs, or in troubling times.

Seeing the big picture makes it easier to recognise which areas of your finances need work, such as scaling back debt, boosting your retirement savings or growing other investments. Once you see the overall view, you can start to build a plan to work towards, and drive, proactive behaviour change. That change will become habit and will also positively impact your mental biases to create sustainable money behaviour.

Knowing where you stand can support better crisis management

Consumers are often advised to manage a crisis – such as rising interest rates or personal job loss – by reviewing their budget. But how can you really plan ahead or know how to handle curveballs if you don't know your starting point?

Having an overarching picture of your wealth can make it a lot less stressful when you encounter life's inevitable glitches. Remember, life isn't perfectly stable or linear – and your career, relationships, living situation and money aren't either.

Knowing your overall wealth picture can prevent knee-jerk responses, and give you confidence that you have the backing of a decent net wealth position to handle difficult situations in a carefully considered way. This, as I have said before, is taking advantage of the real value of money – it gives you financial freedom by gaining you time to make informed choices.

Your goals – not the Joneses'

A recent survey found near enough that one in two Australians have felt pressured by their social circle to spend money. The research showed one in five people have even gone into debt or spent more than they could afford because of the pressure to match the spending of those around them.

Spending out of peer pressure is an easy trap to fall into, but it does your finances no favours. Also, keep in mind what you don't see: the behind-the-scenes reality. A neighbour who just spent a motza renovating their home to showroom standards, or a friend who regularly buys a new car, could be deep in bad debt and living with extreme financial pressure.

When you have a total view of your finances, it is much easier to set goals that are relevant to you and your family. It can also encourage you to think twice about unnecessary spending just to keep up with the Joneses.

Remember, the most important thing should be your goals and your future when it comes to money. You are the only one in control of that destiny. Your peers have their own financial destinies, so leave that to them. In short – don't compete, because your plan is all you need.

How to grasp the big picture

Each year, publicly listed companies are required to produce a set of annual accounts that let shareholders and other parties see the complete picture of the business – warts and all. This overarching view is provided by the company's balance sheet. It shows assets – everything of value the company owns. On the other side of the ledger are liabilities – amounts owed by the company to third parties.

Individuals and households can also produce personal balance sheets. They are a useful tool to help you take a holistic, big-picture view of your finances.

Plenty of apps are available to help you see the overall strength of your financial wellbeing. Your net wealth is something you can work out on paper, just by adding up all your personal assets and subtracting the value of all the debts you owe. The end figure is your 'net' (assets minus liabilities) wealth.

The whole point of the exercise is to discover the true strength of your overall financial position. If your total assets outweigh your debts, you're in front. It's when your total debts add up to more than your total assets that action needs to be taken.

However, as I mentioned earlier, many of us would be pleasantly surprised by the value of our net wealth. Table 10.1 represents a household balance sheet for the average person as at December 2020. If we take a look at the figures, it is clear that owning a home and growing superannuation plus other financial assets can make a real difference to personal wealth.

Sure, the table shows the value of 'other property' ($197,900), which reflects the enthusiasm many people have for investment properties. But it's good to see that 'Other financial assets', which include shares and savings, totals $162,500.

The upshot of the ABS results in the table is that the average Australian household owns $1.2 million worth of assets, while owing less than $200,000 in personal debt. This brings personal net wealth to $1.02 million. Long story short, you could be well off and not even know it!

Table 10.1: Household average wealth – all households

ASSETS	
Financial assets	**$'000**
Total value of superannuation funds	223.7
Value of other financial assets	162.5
Total financial assets	386.2
Property assets	
Value of owner occupied dwelling	533.2
Value of other property	197.9
Total property assets	731.1
Value of other non-financial assets	104.0
Total non-financial assets	835.0
Total assets	**1,221.3**

LIABILITIES	
Principal outstanding on loans for owner occupied home	117.5
Principal outstanding on other property loans	62.2
Total property loans	179.7
Amount owing on credit cards	2.0
Amount owing on other loans	17.7
Total liabilities	**199.3**

NET WORTH OF HOUSEHOLD	**1,021.9**

Source: Australian Bureau of Statistics 2021, 'Household financial resources', abs.gov.au/statistics/economy/finance/household-financial-resources/latest-release.

Seeing your wealth through the lens of your complete financial wellbeing makes it a lot easier to measure your progress. We live in a complex financial world. We are continually called on to make complex money decisions, and it can feel as though we aren't making any real financial progress. It is not until you can climb to the top of the mountain and see the 360-degree view that you realise just how far you have come, how much you have achieved, and how being in the valley below can cloud your perspective.

So, please, go ahead and take a good look at the elephant as a whole. Then apply the same big-picture thinking to your finances. It is a fair bet you'll be impressed with your progress so far and see a clearer path ahead.

Up next, we'll look at how to control those things you *can* control in your life with money.

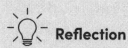 **Reflection**

- Which elements of your finances do you tend to keep track of regularly?
- Which elements do you tend to avoid looking at?
- Have you created your own household balance sheet to view your wealth holistically? (If not, what are you waiting for?)

Chapter 11

Control your controllables

Only you can control your future.
– Dr. Seuss

We all know what we can and can't control in our lives, yet we spend most of our time focusing on what we can't control rather than what we can.

How many times have you wished for a lottery or competition win, or some other unplanned windfall? These are all uncontrollables. They may happen, but the probability is miniscule. However, many of us dream of these outcomes, thinking a mountain of money would make life easier or better.

There's no doubt that a bit of extra cash is always welcome. But instead of pinning your financial future on something you have little control over, and that may never happen at all, it makes more sense to focus on things you can control to boost your financial wellbeing. A simple but foolproof strategy is to control your controllables. That's what this chapter is all about.

The single largest undisputed controllable in your financial arsenal is to save more than you spend. There's nothing new or life-changing in this epiphany – it's just fact.

However, controlling what you spend is the difficult part – particularly if your behaviour and personality with money is based in spending. Remember, though, this book is about helping you put your mind over money. It may be difficult for some money personalities, but it's not impossible. It starts with evaluating your expenses and out-goings. It's not about being a scrooge or living like a hermit. Rather, this strategy focuses on getting 'value for money'.

Interestingly enough, it's often the essentials that need to be addressed first. In the economics and finance world, it is accepted that there are five areas of spending that are classified as 'essential': food, housing, education, health and energy. These are the things you are unlikely to compromise on as they are essential to living. But if you dig a little deeper, you'll find an array of expenses that you may be able to reduce without compromising your living situation.

If you can shift your essentials from making up 100 per cent of your household spending to 60 or 70 per cent, you'll be well on your way to creating savings that will allow you to grow a pool of investments and earn passive income. It's a pathway that lets you earn more without working harder or longer. It means it's possible to turn wishful thinking about having more money into reality.

Control and budgeting

Read any personal finance book or magazine and you're bound to be advised on the merits of budgeting. It's no secret that budgeting can play an important role in keeping spending under control. After all, big companies and governments follow budgets to maintain financial control and prevent money from being wasted. Budgets can work just as well for individuals, too. The catch is that budgeting is restrictive and it requires effort – factors that are serious stumbling blocks for human beings.

Budgets are also a *today* tool, not a tomorrow or beyond tool. There is a narrow time focus in a budget; they are beneficial for providing an understanding of your money for the next week or month or, in some cases, the next year, but in the main they are a short-term loop. They get you to the end of the budget period, then you need to start over. They don't help you break bad habits, and they don't expand your view to your whole money elephant.

I believe these are the reasons many of us fail to stick to a budget. They don't address your controllables. Instead, they put a band-aid over the main issue – your money is controlling your mind, and therefore it's controlling your time and your financial freedom.

This is backed by research showing near enough to three in four Americans follow some sort of budget, yet eight out of 10 have trouble sticking to their own spending limits despite their best efforts. In fact, the study found Americans overspend their budget by about US$7429 every year.

While these figures relate to the US, I suspect they apply just as well here in Australia and to other similar countries. The survey found the biggest budget killers are online shopping, grocery shopping and subscription services. Sound familiar? And, according to the poll, all the usual suspects made it into the top 10 budget busters: buying lunch every day, using food delivery services and having gym memberships.

Why is budgeting so challenging? There are two reasons: spending is more fun than saving (we'll look at this further in chapter 12), and we tend to build a budget based on what we have paid in the past. This is a critical error that can set us up for failure from the get-go.

This is where reorientating your viewpoint needs to kick in – just as your view on volatility in markets needs to be reorientated. The fixed cost expenses that make up the backbone of your budget can easily roll into overspending if you don't keep a close eye on them.

By fixed cost expenses I mean general, health and car insurances; energy bills; loan repayments; and telecommunication bills (internet and phone). Cost increases in these services tend to be small and incremental and you may not register how much of an effect they are having on your overall money position – that's why these providers only make small incremental increases. These increases eat into your today money harder and faster than anything else.

Contract providers are more likely to hit you hard once the first 12 months of your dealings with them have passed. This is where your habits need to change. Allowing legacy contracts to roll over is like compound interest in reverse. Every increase in fees is less money for you. The less money you have to allow for compound interest, the less return you will have over your investment lifetime.

This is why starting with improving your fixed cost expenses is essential to controlling your controllables. Tracking down that better deal cuts your expenses and provides instant spare cash for saving without the need to scrimp on your lifestyle. It makes it easier to achieve the goal of spending less than you earn.

Make a list of all your fixed costs. Include home loan repayments, insurance, power, internet and so on. Note how much you paid for each of these last year, or what you are currently paying if it's a regular outgoing like phone bills and internet subscriptions. This gives you a baseline to work from.

I know this approach requires labour – actual personal labour hours. But it is a necessary step to start forming good habits. It's like exercising: start small then build from there. Look at one cost and fix that. Then look at the second cost and repeat. The amount you can save doing this can add up to become quite substantial over multiple areas of expenditure – and you haven't had to change your lifestyle spending to make these savings, either.

Let's take a closer look at how much you could save by controlling your controllables. We'll go through five key areas where an Australian family could potentially save more than $3000 annually. For a high-income earner that's like landing a $6000 before-tax pay rise.

Home loan

I have a saying I try to live by when it comes to banks: banks are not your friends. Also remember this: banks use compound interest against you. Any loan you have is putting compound interest in reverse. Every time the bank charges interest this increases your overall loan total, meaning it will take you that much longer to pay it off. The only way to reduce the principal is to make sure your repayments are larger than what the bank is deducting in interest.

The average mortgage in Australia is about $500,000. With that sort of balance to play around with there's plenty of scope for an improved interest rate. Even a small reduction in your interest rate can deliver big savings on monthly repayments and a massive reduction in your long-term interest bill.

Data from the Reserve Bank of Australia shows the average variable rate for existing loans across the major banks is 2.89 per cent (as of March 2022). At that rate you'd pay around $2343 in monthly repayments on a $500,000 mortgage with a 25-year loan.

However, the average rate for new loans with smaller lenders is 2.46 per cent. That's a potential rate cut of 0.43 per cent just by switching to a lower-rate lender. On that same $500,000 mortgage, this could see your monthly repayments drop to around $2233. It's a difference that really stacks up, providing a saving of $110 monthly or $1320 annually. For the record, I have used average figures here, but plenty of lenders have even lower rates, so you could save far more with a little shopping around.

There is another way to look at this. Your house is a *beyond* asset – part of your money pool that is for future wealth. If you were to reduce your monthly interest charges but keep your monthly repayments the same, you'd be owning your beyond asset more quickly. The more principal you pay into your housing asset, the lower the mortgage, the lower the interest repayments and the more you actually own. This is saving and investing wrapped into one small change in your spending habits. The power of this can't be overstated. Knowing you will be owning your own home faster creates a confidence and financial security this is referred to as the 'wealth effect'. You will feel wealthier, even though your income has not changed.

Big caveat here: the wealth effect can lead to a confidence that induces spending. When feeling wealthier, people can fall into the trap of spending this additional wealth. Concentrate on the freedom created by owning your own house faster rather than the possible additional spending capacity you have.

Home and car insurance

The cost of insuring our homes has crept up in recent years. Factors like climate change have led to increased levels of wild weather, which has jacked up premiums on home and contents cover – and this isn't set to be resolved any time soon, so these events will continue to occur more often. Nonetheless, as your home is a major asset, this is one expense you can't afford to shrug off. Moreover, having building insurance in place is typically a requirement of most home loans. But this doesn't mean that you have to put up with over-the-top premiums.

In May 2022, the annual cost to insure your home ranges from around $1000 to $1600 depending on the state you live in. Residents in Australia's cyclone-prone north can pay four times this amount, but for now let's stick to the average annual premium of $1400 that applies in New South Wales.

Instead of just allowing your insurance to roll over at renewal time, compare what's available with other insurers. Even if you don't score a lower premium, insurers will typically offer a generous discount on the first year of cover when you organise and arrange a new policy. These discounts can be as high as 30 per cent. That would suggest you could cut a $1400 premium down to $980 – a saving of $420 – just by taking your business elsewhere. That $420 is money you control; money that you have now saved; money that can be used in more productive ways if it's added to an investment that is taking advantage of compound interest. I know that $420 in isolation may not seem like much, but this is just one small saving in a group of savings – add them together and $420 will become $1000 and then some.

As with your home and contents insurance, do not accept the rollover rate for car insurance. Car insurance is one of the worst for increasing in price year on year. That is your money they are taking off you, and I promise you it's going to look better in your pocket than with your insurance provider. Your personal labour in comparing better deals will pay you back.

Health insurance

Private health insurance is not cheap. Nor should it be: medical professionals are highly skilled and should be paid for their expertise, if you unfortunately happen to need it. But there are ways to limit the cost of health insurance.

First, eliminate features in your health insurance you don't need or want, or opt for a higher excess. As with home and car insurance, the biggest savings can come by switching providers. A very close colleague of mine has a perfect saying when it comes to insurers: 'Never get in the way of an insurer and a bag of money.' She is not wrong – which is why if you threaten to take your bag of money away a deal will appear.

Health insurance premiums for a family of four with top-level 'Gold' cover can cost up to $1202 annually. The standard-value product is $577 per annum. That's a whopping $635 saving. Now, you may have better peace of mind with the Gold cover, and thus the 'value' of the cover can be justified, but what else is inside that $1202 premium? Are you truly in control of the cost of your health insurance?

Credit cards

Credit cards are one area where interest rates have remained stubbornly high – even though in recent years we have seen home loan and other personal lending rates hit rock-bottom lows. While there is no shortage of credit cards charging interest of 20 per cent plus, it is possible to more than halve this rate. A number of card issuers, particularly smaller banks and credit unions, have card rates of 8.99 per cent.

Switching a credit card debt of $3000 from a card charging 20 per cent to one costing 8.99 per cent can see you pocket annual savings of $330.

Power providers

If you want to put some real spark in your savings, look no further than your power providers.

Power bills can have a habit of creeping up on us because they are typically paid quarterly rather than annually. If you're in any doubt about how expensive electricity and gas can be, add up your last four quarterly bills to see the annual cost.

On the plus side, most of us now have considerable choice in providers, so you don't have to put up with overpriced electricity.

As an example of the potential savings, a Victorian household could pay the default offer of $1307 annually. Or, they could cut this to as low as $951 with a cheaper provider. That's a saving of $356 annually – more money you now have control over by just controlling your controllable expenditure.

The verdict

The savings I have outlined are summarised in table 11.1. It shows that by cutting back just five of your household's fixed costs, you have the potential to slash $3000 from your annual household budget.

Importantly, this saving doesn't mean skipping nights out with friends, or avocado on toast at your local cafe.

In every instance that I have looked at (besides, possibly, the health insurance cover), you are getting the same product. The difference is that you are paying less. It begs the question: why pay more?

This is just a small sample of what you have in your control to gain financial freedom and reach that goal of saving more and spending less. You will also find that, as you undertake these changes, other personal change will occur. These changes will be specific to you, but acknowledge what they are – you are recognising spending habits and behaviours you think you can control and change for your betterment.

It's your mind taking control over your money.

What we have just discussed has a horrible name – 'lazy tax'. It refers to people paying more, often for the basics, because they can't be bothered putting in some personal labour. The catch, as we've seen here, is that lazy tax isn't nickel and dime stuff.

We all have a variety of fixed costs. They're unavoidable. But you can ease the financial pain by taking advantage of better options. It can put a generous serve of savings in your today money bucket. Once you've made the switch, those savings can be moved to your tomorrow and beyond money buckets, turning your savings into money-returning assets for that financial freedom you are looking for.

Table 11.1: Five ways to cut your consumables and save over $3000 annually

Fixed cost	Current cost	Switching option	Annual saving by switching
Home loan repayments: $500,000 mortgage, 25-year term	Average rate for established loans with major banks: 2.89%* Monthly repayment: $2343	Average rate for new loans with small lenders: 2.46%* Monthly repayment: $2233	$1320
Home insurance	Average annual premium: $1400^	Potential saving just for moving to a new insurer: 30% discount^^	$420
Health insurance: family of four; monthly premium before rebate	Most expensive monthly premium+: $1202	Cheapest monthly premium+: $577	$635
Credit card debt of $3000	High interest rate: 20% Annual interest charge: $600	Low interest rate: 8.99% Annual interest charge: $270	$330
Electricity	Default offer Victoria∞: $1307	Cheapest plan: $951∞	$356
Potential annual savings			$3061

Sources:
* Reserve Bank of Australia 2022, 'Lenders' Interest Rates', rba.gov.au/statistics/interest-rates.
^ Tamika Seeto 2022, 'How much is home and contents insurance?', Canstar, canstar.com.au/home-insurance/home-contents-insurance-cost.
^^ Budget Direct 2022, 'Home Insurance', budgetdirect.com.au/home-contents-insurance.html.
+ PrivateHealth.gov.au 2022, 'Compare policies', privatehealth.gov.au/dynamic/search.
∞ Jared Mullane 2022, 'Compare Cheapest Electricity Prices in Victoria', Canstar Blue, canstarblue.com.au/electricity/cheapest-electricity-prices-victoria.

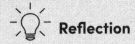 **Reflection**

- Do you tend to dream of getting a windfall, rather than concentrating on things in your control?
- Do you find sticking to a budget challenging? If so, what steps could you put in place to motivate yourself or change your behaviour?
- When was the last time you reviewed your controllables to seek out better deals?

Chapter 12

Spendvesting

I'm not a shopaholic; I'm just helping the economy.
– Anonymous

One trillion dollars – that is how much Australians spent in 2020. Shelter and food do account for a massive chunk of that spend, as do other essential items. But some of the numbers for non-essential spending – 'discretionary' spending – might also make your eyes water.

Figure 12.1 opposite gives a breakdown of the total spending that took place in Australia in 2020. Australians managed to spend $100.5 billion on recreation, $50.6 billion on hotels, cafes and restaurants, a monstruous $24.7 billion on alcohol and $22.4 billion on cigarettes.

Granted, 2020 was a 'special' year. The effects of COVID-19 will be etched into our financial behaviour for decades. The exponential rise in working from home and online shopping created permanent changes to our living and working arrangements. This explains the strong jump in furniture sales to $53.9 billion and $34.6 billion on clothing.

Let me put that comment into perspective: in 2020, online shopping had been around for just over 30 years. In 2019, approximately 20 per cent of all sales occurred online. In 2020, that rose to 27 per cent.

That's a 7 per cent increase in one year, when it had taken 30 years to get to 20 per cent.

Figure 12.1: Australian household expenditure (2020)

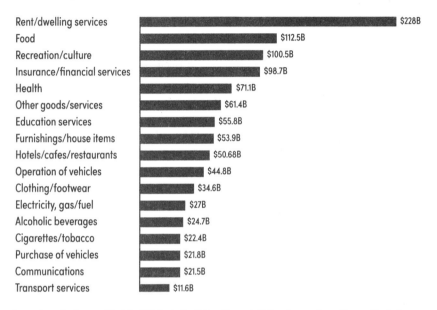

Rent/dwelling services	$228B
Food	$112.5B
Recreation/culture	$100.5B
Insurance/financial services	$98.7B
Health	$71.1B
Other goods/services	$61.4B
Education services	$55.8B
Furnishings/house items	$53.9B
Hotels/cafes/restaurants	$50.68B
Operation of vehicles	$44.8B
Clothing/footwear	$34.6B
Electricity, gas/fuel	$27B
Alcoholic beverages	$24.7B
Cigarettes/tobacco	$22.4B
Purchase of vehicles	$21.8B
Communications	$21.5B
Transport services	$11.6B

Source: Australian Bureau of Statistics 2022, 'Australian National Accounts: National Income, Expenditure and Product', abs.gov.au/statistics/economy/national-accounts/australian-national-accounts-national-income-expenditure-and-product/latest-release.

Australian banking giant Westpac revealed that across Westpac group customers, the median balance across transaction, savings and term deposit accounts at the end of 2020 was an underwhelming $3559. That's a pretty lacklustre sum given that 2020 was the first year of the COVID pandemic and the trend of Australians swinging from net spenders to net savers kicked in around late March that year. Even more worrisome, a ME Bank survey found that in 2022, more than one in five households reported having less than $1000 in cash savings, and 12 per cent of this group had less than $100 in saved cash.

While Australians have become net savers, the savings are still pretty lacklustre. We could all afford to reign in our spending. But how can we keep the spending habit at bay and continue with the good habits around saving we began during the pandemic?

What if we could change our spending habit into an investing habit? What if we became 'spendvestors'?

Think about it. We spend over $1 trillion annually. If we diverted just 10 per cent of that spending – that's just one dollar out of every $10 we spend – into saving and investments, the benefits would be tremendous.

Changing this one habit would immediately put you on the path to financial freedom. You would find that the money you have for today increases, the money you wanted to set aside for tomorrow is actually there and your beyond fund would start to see regular contributions that you could not have made otherwise.

It is possible to turn spending habits into investment habits. The first step is understanding why we are compelled to spend on purchases that often have no lasting value and bring only the briefest flicker of joy into our lives. This is where it really is a case of mind over money.

Why do we spend?

Spending is a stimulator. Numerous research papers have found that making shopping decisions can reinforce a sense of personal control over our environment, and that spending on discretionary items can ease feelings of sadness. This means 'retail therapy' is not just a saying, it is a real psychological phenomenon.

The studies also found that one of the main physiological responses to spending is the release of the neurotransmitter and hormone dopamine. It's common knowledge that dopamine is known as the 'feel-good' or pleasure hormone. What's less understood by most is its function in learning, memory and motor system functioning.

Coupling pleasure with learning and memory explains the link with behaviour. If we remember that spending gives us a 'high' (makes us feel good) we will continue to find ways to repeat that behaviour.

Further research has found that it's not the item itself that brings joy. It is the *anticipation* of making a purchase that delivers a dopamine spike. And that spike is short-lived. As soon as we have paid for the item and left the store, or received the parcel if it's an online purchase, our dopamine levels quickly return to normal. This can be rapidly followed by a sense of regret – buyer's remorse (one in four shoppers admit to feeling regret after buying an item on sale).

Spending can be harmless or even good for you; but just like many things in this world, going to excess leads to bad outcomes. Think about your last discretionary spend: a new outfit or pair of shoes, a second coffee, a sneaky chocolate bar. Whatever your example, if your habit is to buy something, anything, consistently you have a spending habit – which will make saving more than you spend all that more difficult.

Habits are powerful behaviours; they are something you perform routinely. In fact, one word used to define habit is 'automatic'. If habits are your automatic behaviours, you may have concluded that you don't have to think about them. You don't have to weigh up why you are behaving this way because it's what you have learned to do, rightly or wrongly.

It takes discipline to break habits and create new ones. You'll need to confront your biases and put in strategies to change your behaviour. But it's absolutely worth it.

Australians spent $34.6 billion on clothing and footwear in 2020. Think about your own spending on these types of items and the impact this has on your financial wellbeing. Do you really need new clothes? Unfortunately, logic like that is unlikely to shift your thinking, or quell your mind's desire for new things and the dopamine hit you get from shopping. So, let's change tack. What about looking at the amount of waste that is created from clothing? Could this trigger a change in your behaviour?

I raise this because each year Australians buy an average of 27 kilograms of new clothing *per person*. At the same time, we each toss 23 kilograms of clothing into landfill annually.

Really ponder this. What that statistic is saying is that a good portion of our clothing spend is also 'disposable': disposable income that is spent on disposable items. It is no wonder many Australians struggle to save, let alone invest to grow wealth, when value is being lost through waste.

Most of us have been guilty of making impulse buys or over-spending at some stage. A PayPal study found the average Australian notches up just over two impulse buys at a total cost of $110 every quarter. That may not sound like much, but that works out to $440 each year. If we allow 60 years of adult life, that adds up to about $26,400 in impulse buys over a lifetime.

There can be a complex range of triggers behind why we spend on unplanned purchases. Boredom, despair, frustration at work or home, unhappiness in our relationship or life. All can be trigger factors that see us seeking joy from spending.

There can be external triggers, too: the biggest being perceived value and the trap of discount marketing. According to PayPal, two in five Australians (42 per cent) say they have purchased an item using a personalised discount, like 'Get 10 per cent off on your birthday'. Perceived value is also heavily influenced by the never-ending flow of sales. Up to one in five of those surveyed reported sales-related FOMO – the belief they would be 'losing money' if they didn't buy an item on sale. About the same number – 19 per cent – said they were 'addicted' to shopping at sales.

This is clearly detrimental behaviour, but it has deep psychological reasoning. Changing this behaviour is possible, but it will require changed thinking and a level of discipline. Even shopaholics can rein in their spending by being mindful and focusing on their long-term financial security.

So, we know from physiology and psychology that it is the *idea* of making a discretionary purchase that is exciting – for a while at least. And this is what lies at the heart of turning a spending habit into an investing habit. We need to turn the feel-good reaction we get from purchasing items to a feel-good reaction from investing and saving. Let's look at some strategies now.

Set goals to trigger a dopamine hit

The research shows we don't get dopamine from general spending – it must be specific, have a perceived personal value and give us a sense of control.

There are plenty of activities besides spending that give us a surge of dopamine. One of these is making money. Studies have also found that setting personal goals, and achieving them, makes us feel good. That is why we get a sense of satisfaction from writing to-do lists. The closer we get to our goal, the greater the hit of dopamine. This can explain why first homebuyers who have saved long and hard for a deposit can be so elated when they are finally approved for a home loan and buy that house.

The simple act of setting goals around how much you will save and invest each month, quarter or year can provide the same psychological and physiological reward as spending money. If you can get on this path you'll be on your way to redefining your behaviour and building the habit of investing.

Reworking spending to investing is the basis of spendvesting. Visualise it that way: you are spending on your investment, and that should give you a kick. It should also give you a sense of control and the satisfaction that you are taking back your financial freedom.

Put investing on autopilot

It is easy for me to suggest that you turn investing into a habit, but I do know habit change is tough and new habits are easy to break. It helps to use the modern-day tools at your disposal to your advantage to engrain your new behaviour as habit.

One of the simplest ways to create an investment habit is to set up regular contributions from your cash account to your savings account or mortgage offset account. Rather than expecting yourself to manually transfer the money, use automation: it requires less effort and can quickly turn investing from a chore into something meaningful and exciting.

It can be a simple process. You may choose, for instance, to save $100 every month, or consider your average monthly spend on discretionary items and use that amount. It needs to be an amount that is meaningful in value to you so that it triggers the same response you get from spending.

Whatever it is, once you have decided upon the monthly amount, set up an automatic transfer to make it happen.

Harness the benefits of dollar cost averaging

There is an investment strategy benefit to this set-up: dollar cost averaging (DCA).

DCA occurs when you invest consistently without interruption. For example: say you invest $500 every fortnight, month or quarter. You invest this amount regardless of the fluctuations in the investment markets in each time period.

This means that you are buying less of an investment when market (or asset) prices are high, and more when market (asset) prices are down. This will mean over time the average price of your investments will moderate to a better price and the scale of your investment capital will be larger – giving you a higher exposure to the effects of compound interest.

Table 12.1 shows the effect of DCA for an investor who decides to buy $100 worth of the same security each month.

Table 12.1: Example of dollar cost averaging (DCA)

	Share price	Amount invested for the month	Number of shares purchased
January	$25	$100	4
February	$30	$100	3
March	$22	$100	4
April	$20	$100	5
May	$18	$100	5
June	$17	$100	5
July	$15	$100	6
August	$15	$100	6
September	$16	$100	6
October	$20	$100	5
November	$25	$100	4
December	$30	$100	3
Total		$1200	56
Average cost per share		$21.42	

By using DCA, our investor buys the most shares when the share price is lowest, and the least when the security price is highest. After a year, our investor has paid an average share price of $21.42 for a total of 56 shares.

If we look at the December price ($30) as the market value of the security, the value of the holding total is $1680, meaning the capital gain over the year is $480. If the investor had just brought in January at $25 for four shares, the value of their holdings would be $120 come December – a $20 gain. Even if the investor had invested all $1200 in January for 48 shares, their December value would be $1440 – a $240 gain – and the average price per share would remain $25.

After years as an investment professional, I have repeatedly seen a pattern whereby humans rush to buy shares when prices are expensive. Then, the minute the market heads south and share values fall, investors become anxious, and sell out when investment prices are at their lowest. This is a recipe for financial disaster, as the investor is out of market as the opportune time – they're selling at the bottom and buying heavily when value is thin.

DCA gives you a disciplined framework to do the exact opposite. It forces you to buy more when shares are cheap, and buy fewer shares when values are high. It also removes the risk of trying to time the market.

Timing the market is a misnomer as no one can consistently sell at the top and buy at the bottom. There is too much chance involved in this concept, which is why its fails over time – mainly due to people procrastinating over entry and exit point, which leads them to never invest at all, or miss the correct exit.

DCA allows you to ignore market timing as all market movements are treated the same, meaning you can focus on the true meaning of investing: your financial freedom.

Know that every dollar spent takes you further from your goals

We all face multiple temptations to spend – and overspend. Resisting that urge can be hard. But it is important to realise that every short-term purchase, which may deliver a few minutes of satisfaction, takes you a step further from reaching your future financial goals.

To change your thinking and behaviour, try relating your spending to your goals. For example, if you are saving for a new home, how far behind in your timeframe would a $600 Apple Watch set you? Is the time you'll sacrifice worth it? If it is, then there is 'value' in the item; if it isn't, the 'value' goes to your investment. It's a win-win way of looking at it.

There is a double advantage here: a check on your spending, and development discipline. The advantage of discipline is that it is a building block towards creating positive habits.

Experiencing the positive emotions related to growing your wealth can also be a great motivator to stay on track with your goals. Money plays such a tremendous role in our lives, so it's no surprise that it also provokes strong emotional responses. The learned behaviours you have developed over the years are habits that have both positively and negatively impacted your financial freedom.

I hope this chapter has helped you identify your spending habits: why you spend, the reactions you have when spending and its financial and psychological impact. I hope it has also given you some tactics to break your spending habits to form new investing habits that will have positive financial outcomes.

The way we manage money can be a huge enabler. If you can identify how your mind works with spending and identify its triggers, this can put you on the path to your financial freedom. If you can turn the physiological impact of dopamine into the pleasure of investing, you can get one step further.

There are few things more rewarding than sitting back, looking at the value created by financial freedom and thinking 'I did that'. It delivers a sense of reward and accomplishment that can be hard to beat and will deliver a dopamine hit that won't fade.

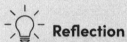 **Reflection**

- How did your spending and saving habits change during the COVID-19 pandemic? Did you begin any good habits that you've now let slide?
- What are your spending cues?
- What steps could you take to put your investing on autopilot?

Chapter 13

Unreasonable expectations

It's your own expectations that hurt you. Not the world
you live in. Whatever happens in the world is real.
What you think should happen is unreal. People are hurt by
their expectations. You're not disappointed by the world,
you are disappointed by your own projections.
– Jacque Fresco

I have always loved this quote. It's a synopsis of the biggest issue we all face – not just with our expectations around money, but around all things we do. We have unreasonable expectations, and this leads to unreasonable failing. In many cases it's a failing you should never experience, as what you were expecting was never possible in the first place.

I can pinpoint the moment I started to use the phrase 'you are you and I am me'. I was giving a presentation to an Australian investment association. I always enjoy giving these talks as the people are engaged and are likely to challenge my points of view, which makes me sharper (and hopefully them too). However, I also know that these presentations are a hive for people with expectations that are either highly risky or just straight-out impossible.

At the end of this particular presentation, a very nice man approached me and asked me about an investment scheme he wanted to invest in. I am not going to name the investment scheme, but know that it has high risk and is opaque in its workings. The man said, 'It's offering a guaranteed 5.5 per cent per annum yield on a deposit of $10,000 or more. What do you think?'

He had a certain look in his eye which told me he had already made his mind up and was going to invest; but his confirmation bias was kicking in, and he wanted someone to give him the tick of approval. I wasn't going to help him, as I could see the investment was not something that he was fully across. I responded: 'You are you I am me – what is best for you may not be best for me, and vice versa – so I can't really make a suggestion either way. But, can I ask, why you are interested in this investment option?'

His answer makes me nervous every time I recount it: 'Because it will give me the yield I need. I need this money to earn as much as it can in the next six months without any risk. I am retiring then and will use the money to travel the world for the next few years.'

They key words in his response are 'without any risk'. All investment has risk; from the simplest cash investment to the top of the risk-reward scale, there is always some risk. The further up the risk-reward scale, the bigger the return, but the higher the chance of loss. A 5.5 per cent term deposit at the time was some 4 to 4.5 per cent above the market, which should highlight that this investment had a level of risk well above equivalent offerings. I also knew that this kind of offering had early break clauses that would see him earn nothing if he wanted to get out of the investment before the agreed term.

Here's a fact: we all want to earn the highest possible return on our money. And another: most people overestimate the returns they can earn on investments.

There is something about the idea of making the most amount of money in the least possible time (often with minimum effort) that strongly resonates with human beings. Quite simply, a quick buck appeals to us. It's what we discussed in chapter 7 around the hyperbolic discounting effect. This is unfortunately why gambling is so addictive: the 'promise' of a quick buck with minimal effort and an unreasonable belief of an abnormal return.

Have a look at some of these truly horrible numbers. In the first five months of 2022 the online gambling market raked in US$59 billion (A$83.8 billion) globally. That is nearly double Apple's operating profit for the March quarter of 2022, which was US$29.9 billion (A$42.7 billion). It is estimated that in 2023 that figure will be US$92.9 billion (A$132.7 billion). On average, Australians spend $1.9 billion on lotto every year. In the US that figure is about US$80 billion (A$114 billion).

Ask yourself: how many people do you know personally who have won a significant amount through gambling or formal lotteries? Chances are it is a very round number – as in zero. That's because our odds of winning a life-changing payout are incredibly small.

All of this comes back to the concepts of delayed return, hyperbolic discounting and short-term biases.

Investing requires discipline, time and accepting gradual returns. The problem, as some investors see it, is that they don't receive high enough returns fast enough. That's why they turn to options that offer the *chance* to reach high returns in unrealistic timeframes.

As soon as you put money into a vehicle that involves chance, it is not an investment – it is a bet.

A study by Schroders revealed just how unrealistic these expectations can be. It found that globally close to two out of five investors (37 per cent) expect annual returns of between 10 and 20 per cent. More than one in 10 respondents (13 per cent) expect returns to top 20 per cent annually. That is, they expect returns that are nearly double the average yearly return of the S&P 500 over the last 10 years (which was 10.9 per cent). (An additional caveat here is that those

10 years included the longest bull market in the S&P 500's 150-plus-year history.)

What the Schroders findings show is that about half the world's investors expect, at a minimum, a return of 10 per cent or more on their investments *every year*. That's an unreasonable expectation.

These were not one-off findings. A 2021 international survey by investment manager Natixis found investors expect to earn long-term returns of 14.5 per cent *above inflation*. US investors were found to have the highest long-term return expectations at 17.5 per cent over inflation. This figure would actually be close to 20 per cent as the average rate of inflation in the US over the last 20 years has been around 2 to 2.5 per cent.

The dangers of unrealistic expectations

Having unrealistically high expectations of investment returns poses serious traps for investors. It can bring consequences that go beyond disappointment. It can create dangerous investment behaviour.

Growth assets such as equities have a track record of high long-term returns. This can see investors concentrating their investments into the higher-risk assets with only limited exposure to less volatile investments. In their quest to chase the unreasonable, investors can enter investments that are outside their risk tolerance, perhaps even investing in euphoria schemes (such as GameStop or buy now pay later equities) or even move from investment into speculation.

I have deliberately tried to avoid talking about speculative investments. Speculation brings in so many emotions, behaviours and traits, making it very difficult to define why we gravitate to speculation. I have touched on some of these behaviours, but the catch with speculation is that people you would normally think would be averse to speculating do so, while those you would expect to speculate don't.

This brings us to cryptocurrencies. In recent years, plenty of investors globally have turned to cryptocurrencies in the hope of pocketing supersized gains. More than one million Australians now own cryptocurrencies such as Bitcoin, Ethereum, Ripple, Cardano and Dogecoin, and the average holding is quite substantial at $20,000.

The downside of digital currencies is that they are purely speculative. They are not backed by anything tangible and they don't generate anything productive. What you are effectively buying is hope – hope that the next person will pay more for the hope and the next person will pay more after that – which by definition is speculation.

It also falls under the greater fool theory, which says that there is always a greater fool willing to pay a higher price for an already overvalued asset due to need or inflation. In other words, every object has a price that is governed by the demand of a specific consumer and not by its intrinsic value. Therefore, buying an overvalued item will give you a return in the future by selling to another person – the greater fool. That really is what crypto has become in its current form.

You would think this would deter investors, but no. The appeal undoubtedly lies in the way digital currencies have at times recorded spectacular gains. In 2021, for example, the value of Bitcoin climbed from US$29,800 in July to US$69,000 just a few months later in November. These are incredible gains. However, as I write in mid-2022, Bitcoin has plummeted to about US$20,000 and has been as low as US$18,500. Plenty of investors, especially those who bought into the market after the November peak, have lost money, possibly plenty of it, on hope – hope of an unreasonable level of return.

I have no idea where digital currencies are heading. No one does. But the issue remains: no matter which vehicle you use for speculation to gain return, loss will be close at hand.

Unrealistic expectations also open investors up to the risk of scams. If your expectations are skewed to the upside, it's a lot harder to spot a scam until it's too late. The prospect of big gains sucks people in. A UK study, for instance, found that only one in three investors (35 per cent) would avoid opportunities that promised over-the-top returns in case of scams.

The Australian Competition and Consumer Commission (ACCC) reported that investment scams fleeced Australians of more than $70 million in the first half of 2021 alone. For the record, more than half of those losses were to cryptocurrency scams. This led the ACCC to urge investors to be on the lookout for so-called investments promising high returns, especially if they are coupled with apparent low risks.

What are realistic returns?

What, then, is the sort of return we can reasonably expect on our investments?

Caveats first: past returns are no guide for future returns, and the examples used here are conventional investments that have the backing of a well-regulated environment designed to maximise investor protections.

If we look across the conventional asset classes of cash, property, Australian equities and international equities, returns vary widely depending on where you invest and for how long. These are summarised in table 13.1.

The low-risk, low-return asset of cash, for example, has yielded an annual return of 1.73 per cent over the last 10 years.

Moving further up the risk curve to listed commercial property, average annual gains sit at 11.5 per cent over the last 10 years. Bear in mind that property has experienced some interesting price swings in the post-COVID environment.

Australian equities, which are the highest-yielding equities in the developed world with solid overall returns, sit further up the risk curve again. Over the last three, five and 10-year periods investors have pocketed total returns averaging between 7.1 per cent and 10.4 per cent annually.

At the upper end of the risk scale sit global shares. For this example, I have used the 23 other developed equities markets (excluding Australia) as ranked by MSCI. As a group they are regarded as a higher-risk investment than Australian equities, owing to the additional risks imposed by factors such as currency movements and geopolitical issues. However, if you were to look at some of them individually, they may be lower in risk than Australian equities. The higher risk is reflected in higher returns. Global shares have recorded returns averaging slightly more than 10 per cent annually over the last three, five and 10-year periods.

Table 13.1: Long-term annualised returns – conventional asset classes

Asset class	3 years	5 years	10 years
Cash*	0.35%	0.95%	1.73%
Australian commercial property^^	5.82%	6.55%	11.49%
Australian shares – total returns** (capital growth plus dividends)	7.08%	8.63%	10.37%
Global shares (ex Australia) – gross returns^	10.98%	10.82%	10.79%

Returns as at May 2022
Sources:
* RBA Bank accepted Bills 90 Days; Morningstar 2022, 'Market Index Returns Base Currency', cdn.morningstar.com.au/mca/s/documents/Index-Return-April-2022.pdf.
^^ MSCI Australia Real Estate Index (AUD).
** S&P/ASX 200.
^ MSCI World ex-Australia Index (USD).

Returns on equities, as you would expect, are higher over the long term due to the higher risk they attract. That risk is more than made up for by the average yearly returns, which should satisfy return expectations. However, as discussed throughout this book, that risk level can be unacceptable to investors, as the mere prospect of loss or an investment that is seen as too unpredictable leads to inaction and money conservatism. Yet, these same individuals expect abnormal returns for 'no risk'.

How can this thought process be explained? Think back to availability bias and its close cousin, recency bias. Recency bias is where we see positive or negative recent events as the most likely long-term outcome. In behavioural finance recency bias presents as the disconnect between expectations and actual returns on investments. Investors may have seen positive returns under previous conditions (for example, during the COVID-19 pandemic) and assume better returns are achievable under better conditions (post-COVID).

It's also likely due to the element of human nature that says we want more, and we want it sooner.

There is another part to this debate: whether you take action under real or theorical situations. When you are 'investing under theory' – that is, you 'know' you can get 10 per cent per annum by investing in a theoretical fund – there is no mental stress on you. The action under these conditions is simple and straightforward, and the fund will give you said return for no risk.

However, when real action is required – actually putting physical capital into the fund – the mental stress of potential loss, regret and error causes inaction. Plus, no investment moves in a linear, one-way, upward direction. So why do we expect this?

Keep it real, keep to a plan, know the risks

Let me stress: as investors, we all want to earn high returns. However, there is no escaping market theory of the risk-reward scale. It is one of the set-in-stone rules of investing.

Having realistic expectations around investment returns matters. You must get your mind around this aspect of money management. It is about more than being able to recognise a scam or ultra-high-risk speculative investment.

Knowing what is a reasonable and achievable return for a particular asset class allows you to set a suitable investment timeframe and decide on the appropriate mix of assets to protect your portfolio against strong downward swings in any one investment or market class. Ultimately, it comes down to finding the blend of risk and return that you are comfortable with.

If you come across an investment promising expectational gains, expect the equivalent in risk. It all comes back to the old mantra, 'if it looks too good to be true, it probably is'. When you know what realistic returns look like, you're in a much better position to sort the spin from reality.

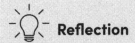 **Reflection**

- Have you ever been tempted by an investment offering high returns with low risk?
- What is your appetite for risk?
- What returns could you reasonably expect given your appetite for risk and financial goals?

Final thoughts

Our minds and money

Money is a terrible master but an excellent servant.
– PT Barnum

When I first set out to write this book, my number-one aim was to demonstrate that no one-size-fits-all approach to money exists. That's because we are all different, with different needs, lives, upbringings, interests, cultures and everything in between.

I certainly think there are strategies and rules that will make your money goals more achievable, but I don't believe one person has found the ultimate best method or approach. That's because there is no one right way – there are multiple options and scenarios, because you, me, us and them are all striving for different things in different timeframes with different amounts of money.

One of the biggest things I've learned in my career to date is that many people don't fully understand what they are striving for, because they haven't really stopped to think about their own beliefs, biases, relationships or culture, and where their money fits in. I hope this book has inspired you to think deeply about these things.

Let me finish this book by telling you a bit more about my money situation and how I have adapted my money behaviour by understanding my biases, habits, personality and relationships.

Me to us

When 'me' becomes 'us' something automatically changes in your behaviour.

I now know that my behaviour, personality and relationship with money in my younger years and early career was purely about serving me. My decision-making, saving and spending was, in full honesty, selfish. And that was fine: it was the right way to be at the time.

Back then, my money only had one thing to do: support my interests and my wants. The catch was that it also meant I had no concept of time. I didn't see the reasoning of thinking past the now, as tomorrow and beyond were just that – beyond my thinking. My biases and personality were not ready to acknowledge the change needed. That was until me became us.

When my now wife and I moved in together it was the first time I was jolted into addressing my money, because it was no longer just *my* money: it was *ours*.

Before I go on, please realise that for us, using our money together is what is best for us. We have always seen everything we do with money, investing and our financial freedom as a joint endeavour. You may be different and that is good. If that means you separate your finances for certain things, please do that. Our way is our way; it is definitely not for everyone.

We also realised we were slightly different when it came to money. My wife isn't as interested in investing as I am, which shouldn't be surprising; I am not as interested in the law as she is, which is also not surprising.

However, we did recognise common traits and biases that allowed us to adapt our thinking and behaviour. From this point we found that we shared the values of family, autonomy and financial stability.

This was a really important realisation for us. It immediately shifted our viewpoint, as we both realised that we needed to think about what *us* meant from a money perspective. We both wanted our children to prosper through education and life experience; we both wanted to live in a house we owned; and we both wanted to be financially comfortable. Not Warren Buffett rich or even super rich – financially comfortable to a point where money allowed us financial freedom.

We were triggered into starting to work towards these goals when we moved to Melbourne. It was a new situation that changed our behaviour and our culture as we got good new jobs, made new friends and were completely financially independent.

This change also created new habits as we were looking towards that next phase of our life: buying a house. We began to save more and started to invest more. I will point out that we still lived a lifestyle we liked – we had avocado on toast and sit-down coffees, drove to the country for the weekend and had the odd overseas trip. It's just that we never did these things to excess, because that was our personality. The thing that changed was what our 'tomorrow' money was being saved for.

We have friends and family members who do things differently. As their salaries increased, they also moved up the 'lifestyle spectrum' – and that works for them, as it's their financial goal. It's not ours, but we don't judge – even though there is a psychological nag that we could. Our goals belong to us; their goals belong to them. It can be liberating to accept that you can be happy with your goals and with your friends' goals too, even though they are different to yours.

We also never compromise each other's financial freedoms because we know that we are in the habit of being net savers. So, if one month there is a higher level of spending than normal, that is fine. And even then, we know it would be very rare to outspend what we save in that period.

This means our today money keeps us ahead, allowing us to diversify our funds for tomorrow and beyond. For instance, the moment our first daughter was born, I set up a fund to achieve the goal of providing her with the life and educational experiences we want her to have. It's tomorrow's money in our goals. We add to this fund regularly – usually once a quarter, although I acknowledge we should probably do it every month. We have just had our second daughter and have done exactly the same thing. Because we are in the habit of adding to our first daughter's fund, it won't be difficult to get into the habit of adding to the second's.

These savings are going to be for everything the girls might need until they are 18: travel, education, special events and so on. Whatever is left after their schooling we want to give to them so they can start their journeys. Again, this is our goal for our money – you may agree or disagree with what we are doing, and that is perfectly fine, because they are not your goals and nor should they be.

Knowing that we have the girls' educational set-up well underway gives me a massive sense of pride. It must be the same pride my parents' felt for my sister and me – the difference being they had to really struggle through that period because they weren't prepared for the challenges the world can give you from time to time.

This is my learned behavioural experience and I have always been aware of its effects on my thinking. I am also lucky in that what was a difficult period resulted in positive outcomes. Knowing that our family will be financially independent is fundamental to my psychology.

We do have a mortgage on our house, and that is also okay. I continuously review it because I secretly enjoy looking for better options. That's just me. I have fixed our loan, unfixed it, refixed it, split it and had it on variable. My reasoning is I am making sure compound interest is working for us, not against us. We overpay our monthly repayments as I know the more we pay off, the more we own, and in my mind that is the most important thing.

That asset is a big part of our money elephant and is part of our beyond assets. We also get the advantage of 'living in our money', if you will. The house is filled with our memories, and we get to have that joy. But we are also aware that if a shock were to come, we are ahead in repayments, ahead in our ownership and ahead in our goals, and we could absorb the challenge.

The true beyond asset for us is our retirement savings. In Australia our retirement funds are locked up by a government mandate, and that is fine with me. It's money that is waiting for us. That wait, however, requires me to almost double my current age, which seems like a lot – but in money terms it really isn't. This is why at the end of every financial year we try to max out what we can contribute to our superannuation.

I also deliberately look at the amount in our retirement savings every few months, just to reorientate my mind. It reminds me that it's out there working and waiting for us when beyond becomes tomorrow and then now. It helps me fight that urge we all have – to make a rash decision when the shocks come. The other advantage is it really does give us time for the eighth wonder of the world – compound interest – to work. If your working life is 45 years, at a conservative compound rate of 5 per cent you will earn over 840 per cent in that time, and that doesn't include additional deposits. This is the beauty of beyond.

The final change to my money behaviour was learning simplicity. By simplicity I mean having one goal and a simple means to get there. When it was just me, I was investing in individual equities, had complex investment strategies and was using additional tools as well. That just couldn't fly as *me* became *us* and *us* became a family of four.

There is not enough time in the day to keep this up, and that is my time. Time is too valuable for complexity. We have enough of that in our lives; we don't need more of it in our money.

We restructured and now have a core group of simple, low-cost ETFs. These are set to reinvest all distributions and dividends, and we use compound interest as much as we can. I break my own rules from time to time by adding in the odd equity here and there, but this is more a plaything for me – and they only make up 10 per cent of our overall listed investments. I also make sure I tell my wife about these, as everything is done jointly.

I know that index investing means we are tying ourselves to the market's performance and that we are not going to outperform. But I also know that on average we should see about 9 to 10 per cent per annum over the next decade, and I would argue that is more than reasonable. In fact, it's better than reasonable: it's very good for what we are trying to achieve, which is financial freedom.

I allow DCA to take effect too by ignoring what the price of the markets is today or tomorrow. I just add in what we have allocated to our tomorrow and beyond funds at the price that is there on that day. That might mean a higher price, which is good as our overall position will have improved. Or it could be lower, in which case the number of units purchased will be greater, meaning we have a bigger pool of funds earning returns in either interest or dividends, and which will be reinvested to help with compounding long term.

None of this is perfect. No one strategy is, because if there was a perfect strategy everyone would do it. But for us, it works. It means our time is ours, our money works for us and we have a freedom now and into the future that makes us happy.

In other words, our minds are in control of our money; and if our minds are over our money, we have financial freedom.

At least, that's our goal. You are you.

References

Chapter 1. To be human is to be reasonable

Bill Bryson 2004, *A Short History of Nearly Everything*, Broadway Books.

Simon Neubauer, Jean-Jacques Hublin & Philipp Gunz 2018, 'The evolution of modern human brain shape', *Science Advances,* vol. 4, no. 1.

Principal 2018, 'We make 35,000 decisions per day, but 7 in 10 postpone major financial decisions', principal.com/about-us/news-room/news-releases/we-make-35000-decisions-day-7-10-postpone-major-financial-decisions.

Alan Watts n.d., 'Choice', Life Eternal, youtube.com/watch?v=D7CH9cRN8Rg.

John Stuart Mill c. 1829–1830, 'On the Definition of Political Economy and Method of Investigation Proper to It'.

Herbert A Simon 1957, *Models of Man: Social and Rational*, Wiley.

Timm Beichelt 2021, *Homo Emotionalis: Zur Systematisierung Von Gefuhlen in Der Politik*, Springer VS.

Chapter 2. You are you, I am me

John Locke 1690, *An Essay Concerning Human Understanding*.

Chapter 3. Money cognition

Baler Bilgin 2012, 'Losses loom more likely than gains: Propensity to imagine losses increases their subjective probability', *Organizational Behavior and Human Decision Processes*, vol. 118, no. 2, pp. 203–215.

Daniel Kahneman & Amos Tversky 1979, 'Prospect Theory: An Analysis of Decision under Risk', *Econometrica*, vol. 47, no. 2, pp. 263–291.

ASX 2020, 'ASX Australian Investor Study 2020', www2.asx.com.au/blog/australian-investor-study.

James Clear n.d., 'The Evolution of Anxiety: Why We Worry and What to Do About It', jamesclear.com/evolution-of-anxiety.

Australian Bureau of Statistics 2021, 'Residential Property Price Indexes: Eight Capital Cities', abs.gov.au/statistics/economy/price-indexes-and-inflation/residential-property-price-indexes-eight-capital-cities/latest-release.

Michael Lynn, Sean Masaki Flynn & Chelsea Helion 2013, 'Do consumers prefer round prices? Evidence from pay-what-you-want decisions and self-pumped gasoline purchases', *Journal of Economic Psychology*, vol. 36, pp. 96–102.

Australian Institute of Health and Welfare 2021, 'Gambling in Australia', aihw.gov.au/reports/australias-welfare/gambling.

Oz Lotteries n.d., 'Powerball', ozlotteries.com/powerball.

Kelsey Munro 2018, 'How safe is flying? Here's what the statistics say', SBS News, sbs.com.au/news/article/how-safe-is-flying-heres-what-the-statistics-say/knzczab06.

National Safety Council 2022, 'Odds of dying', injuryfacts.nsc.org/all-injuries/preventable-death-overview/odds-of-dying.

Brad M Barber & Terrance Odean 2007, 'All That Glitters: The Effect of Attention and News on the Buying Behavior of Individual and Institutional Investors', *The Review of Financial Studies*, vol. 21, no. 2, pp. 785–818.

Daniel Kahneman 1973, *Attention and Effort*, Prentice-Hall.

Chapter 4. The five money personalities

Dr David Whitebread and Dr Sue Bingham 2013, 'Habit Formation and Learning in Young Children', Money Advice Service, maps.org.uk/wp-content/uploads/2021/03/mas-habit-formation-and-learning-in-young-children-executive-summary.pdf.

Craig E Smith, Margaret Echelbarger, Susan A Gelman & Scott I Rick 2017, 'Spendthrifts and Tightwads in Childhood: Feelings about Spending Predict Children's Financial Decision Making', *Journal of Behavioral Decision Making*, vol. 31, no. 3, pp. 446–460.

Sumit Agarwal, Slava Mikhed & Barry Scholnick 2018, 'Peers' Income and Financial Distress: Evidence from Lottery Winners and Neighboring Bankruptcies', Federal Reserve Bank Philadelphia, philadelphiafed.org/consumer-finance/consumer-credit/peers-income-and-financial-distress-evidence-from-lottery-winners-and-neighboring-bankruptcies.

Scott I Rick, Beatriz Pereira & Katherine A Burson 2014, 'The benefits of retail therapy: Making purchase decisions reduces residual sadness', *Journal of Consumer Psychology*, vol. 24, no. 3, pp. 373–380.

UNSW Business School 2018, 'Stash or flash: What makes some people savers and other people spenders?', businessthink.unsw.edu.au/articles/people-spending-saving.

American Psychological Association 2015, 'Stress in America – Paying With Our Health', apa.org/news/press/releases/stress/2014/stress-report.pdf.

Chapter 5. When money collides

Ramsey 2018, 'Money Ruining Marriages in America: A Ramsey Solutions study', ramseysolutions.com/company/newsroom/releases/money-ruining-marriages-in-america.

Kelly Emmerton 2018, 'It's not you, it's your bank account: Australia's biggest financial relationship deal breakers', Mozo, mozo.com.au/personal-loans/articles/biggest-financial-relationship-deal-breakers.

Australian Bureau of Statistics 2021, 'Marriages and Divorces, Australia', abs.gov.au/statistics/people/people-and-communities/marriages-and-divorces-australia/latest-release.

Matt Garrett n.d., 'Do couples separate because of financial difficulties – Yes and No', Relationships Australia NSW, relationshipsnsw.org.au/do-couples-separate-because-of-financial-difficulties-yes-and-no.

Chapter 6. Liberation: the reality of choice

Karen Salmansohn 2011, 'The No. 1 Contributor to Happiness', Psychology Today, psychologytoday.com/au/blog/bouncing-back/201106/the-no-1-contributor-happiness.

Chapter 7: Time heals all

SH Chung & RJ Herrnstein 1967, 'Choice and delay of Reinforcement', *Journal of the Experimental Analysis of Behavior*, vol. 10.

David Laibson 1997, 'Golden Eggs and Hyperbolic Discounting', *Quarterly Journal of Economics*, vol. 112, no. 2, pp. 443–477.

David Laibson 1994, 'Self-Control and Saving'.

George-Marios Angeletos, David Laibson, Andrea Repetto, Jeremy Tobacman & Stephen Weinberg 2001, 'The Hyperbolic Consumption Model: Calibration, Simulation, and Empirical Evaluation', *Journal of Economic Perspectives*, vol. 15, no. 3, pp. 47–68.

MoneySmart 2022, 'Mortgage calculator', moneysmart.gov.au/home-loans/mortgage-calculator.

Mei Wang, Marc Oliver Rieger & Thorsten Hens 2015, 'How Time Preferences Differ: Evidence from 53 Countries', *Journal of Economic Psychology*, vol. 52, no. 4.

Chapter 8. Money culture

Longmei Zhang et. al. 2018, 'China's High Savings: Drivers, Prospects, and Policies', International Monetary Fund, imf.org/-/media/Files/Publications/WP/2018/wp18277.ashx.

European Central Bank 2020, 'Study on the payment attitudes of consumers in the euro area (SPACE)', ecb.europa.eu/pub/pdf/other/ecb.spacereport202012~bb2038bbb6.en.pdf.

Geert Hofstede 2011, 'Dimensionalizing Cultures: The Hofstede Model in Context', *Online Readings in Psychology and Culture*, vol. 2, no. 1.

Mei Wang, Marc Oliver Rieger & Thorsten Hens 2016, 'The Impact of Culture on Loss Aversion', *Journal of Behavioral Decision Making*, vol. 30, no. 2.

Dr Thorsten Hens & Anna Meier 2016, 'Behavioral finance: The psychology of investing', CreditSuisse, credit-suisse.com/media/assets/private-banking/docs/mx/wp-07-behavioral-finance-en.pdf.

Chapter 9. Loving the scary ugly

Lance Hosey 2013, 'Why We Love Beautiful Things', *The New York Times*, nytimes.com/2013/02/17/opinion/sunday/why-we-love-beautiful-things.html.

Karen McVeigh 2009, 'Why golden ratio pleases the eye: US academic says he knows art secret', *The Guardian*, theguardian.com/artanddesign/2009/dec/28/golden-ratio-us-academic.

Chia-Shu Lin, Ching-Yi Wu, Shih-Yun Wu & Hsiao-Han Lin 2018, 'Brain activations associated with fearful experience show common and distinct patterns between younger and older adults in the hippocampus and the amygdala', *Scientific Reports*, vol. 8.

University of Maryland School of Medicine 2018, 'Scientists identify connection between dopamine and behavior related to pain and fear', ScienceDaily, sciencedaily.com/releases/2018/04/180419131108.htm.

Harry Markowitz 1952, 'Portfolio Selection', *The Journal of Finance*, vol. 7, no. 1, pp. 77–91.

Gur Huberman 2001, 'Familiarity Breeds Investment', *The Review of Financial Studies*, vol. 14, no. 3, pp. 659–680.

Australian Securities Exchange 2020, 'ASX Australian Investor Study 2020', www2.asx.com.au/content/dam/asx/blog/ASX-Australian-Investor-Study-2020-Issuers-Report.pdf.

Chapter 10. The elephant paradigm

Natascha Kwiet-Evans 2022, 'Unattainable wealth aspirations: Average Aussie needs $330,000 to feel rich', Finder, finder.com.au/average-aussie-needs-330000-to-feel-rich.

Australian Bureau of Statistics 2021, 'Household financial resources', abs.gov.au/statistics/economy/finance/household-financial-resources/latest-release.

Sophie Wallis 2022, 'Financial peer pressure', Finder, finder.com.au/financial-peer-pressure.

Chapter 11. Control your controllables

Cision 2019, 'Americans Spend $7,429.24 Over Their Budget Every Year, According to New Survey Commissioned by Slickdeals', prnewswire.com/news-releases/americans-spend-7-429-24-over-their-budget-every-year-according-to-new-survey-commissioned-by-slickdeals-300919639.html.

Australian Bureau of Statistics 2022, 'Lending indicators', abs.gov.au/statistics/economy/finance/lending-indicators/latest-release.

Reserve Bank of Australia 2022, 'Lenders' Interest Rates', rba.gov.au/statistics/interest-rates.

Tamika Seeto 2022, 'How much is home and contents insurance?', Canstar, canstar.com.au/home-insurance/home-contents-insurance-cost.

Budget Direct 2022, 'Home Insurance', budgetdirect.com.au/home-contents-insurance.html.

PrivateHealth.gov.au 2022, 'Compare policies', privatehealth.gov.au/dynamic/search.

Jared Mullane 2022, 'Compare Cheapest Electricity Prices in Victoria', Canstar Blue, canstarblue.com.au/electricity/cheapest-electricity-prices-victoria.

Chapter 12. Spendvesting

Australian Bureau of Statistics 2022, 'Australian National Accounts: National Income, Expenditure and Product', abs.gov.au/statistics/economy/national-accounts/australian-national-accounts-national-income-expenditure-and-product/latest-release.

A Selin Atalay & Margaret G Meloy 2011, 'Retail therapy: A strategic effort to improve mood', vol. 28, no. 6, pp. 638–659.

Business Wire 2013, 'Ebates Survey: More Than Half (51.8%) of Americans Engage in Retail Therapy– 63.9% of Women and 39.8% of Men Shop to Improve Their Mood', businesswire.com/news/home/20130402005600/en/Ebates-Survey-More-Than-Half-51.8-of-Americans-Engage-in-Retail-Therapy%E2%80%94-63.9-of-Women-and-39.8-of-Men-Shop-to-Improve-Their-Mood.

Susan Weinschenk 2015, 'Shopping, Dopamine, and Anticipation: What monkeys have to teach us about shopping', Psychology Today, psychologytoday.com/au/blog/brain-wise/201510/shopping-dopamine-and-anticipation.

PayPal 2021, 'PayPal research shows younger Australians are strategic sales shoppers, but risk over doing it', newsroom.au.paypal-corp.com/PayPal_research_shows_younger_Australians_are_strategic_sales_shoppers,-but-risk-over-doing-it.

Westpac 2020, 'Savings by age', westpac.com.au/personal-banking/solutions/budgeting-and-savings/savings/savings-by-age.

ME Bank 2022, 'The average Australian household is as financially comfortable as ever, but long-term outlook is gloomy', mebank.com.au/news/the-average-australian-household-is-as-financially.

Department of Climate Change, Energy, the Environment and Water 2021, 'Clothing textiles waste', dcceew.gov.au/environment/protection/waste/product-stewardship/textile-waste-roundtable.

Ethan S Bromberg-Martin, Masayuki Matsumoto & Okihide Hikosaka 2010, 'Dopamine in motivational control: rewarding, aversive, and alerting', *Neuron*, vol. 68, no. 5, pp. 815–834.

Health Direct n.d., 'Dopamine', healthdirect.gov.au/dopamine.

Ralph Ryback 2016, 'The Science of Accomplishing Your Goals', Psychology Today, psychologytoday.com/au/blog/the-truisms-wellness/201610/the-science-accomplishing-your-goals.

Nick Wolny 2021, 'Why you love setting goals more than pursuing them, according to science', Fast Company, fastcompany.com/90662001/why-you-love-setting-goals-more-than-pursuing-them-according-to-science.

Chapter 13. Unreasonable expectations

Apple 2022, 'Apple Reports Second-Quarter Results', apple.com/au/newsroom/2022/04/apple-reports-second-quarter-results.

Statista 2022, 'Market size of the online gambling industry worldwide from 2019 to 2023', statista.com/statistics/270728/market-volume-of-online-gaming-worldwide.

Oz Lotteries n.d., 'Exactly How Much Do Australians Win On Gambling?', ozlotteries.com/blog/how-much-do-australians-win-on-gambling.

Chris Isidore 2017, 'We spend billions on lottery tickets. Here's where all that money goes', CNNMoney, money.cnn.com/2017/08/24/news/economy/lottery-spending/index.html.

References

Schroders 2017, 'Global Investor Study 2017', prod.schroders.com/en/
sysglobalassets/digital/insights/2017/pdf/global-investor-study-2017/
theme2/schroders_report-2__eng_master.pdf.

Dave Goodsell 2021, '2021 Global Survey of Individual Investors',
Natixis, im.natixis.com/au/research/2021-natixis-global-survey-of-
individual-investors.

Roy Morgan 2022, 'Over 1 million Australians now own
Cryptocurrencies such as Bitcoin, Ethereum, Ripple, Cardano, Dogecoin
and Shiba Inu', roymorgan.com/findings/8929-cryptocurrency-
february-2022-202204120119.

Coinbase 2022, 'Bitcoin price', coinbase.com/price/bitcoin.

Aegon 2021, 'Low interest rates have prompted huge numbers of people
to invest – but unrealistically high expectations of returns may leave
some open to scams', aegon.co.uk/content/ukpaw/news/low_interest_
rateshavepromptedhugenumbersofpeopletoinvestbutunre.html.

Australian Competition and Consumer Commission 2021, 'Australians
lose over $70 million to bogus investment opportunities', accc.gov.au/
media-release/australians-lose-over-70-million-to-bogus-investment-
opportunities.

Glossary

Anchoring: Using a first impression to give a baseline or anchor point as to how to interact and behave.

Asset: A resource that has economic value to an individual, company or country as it provides future benefit.

Attention bias: Where you pay attention to some things while simultaneously ignoring others.

Availability bias: The perception of the likelihood of something happening based off the evidence that first comes to mind.

Bad debt: The debt on assets that have negative appreciation (such as vehicles, travel or apparel) and high rates of interest. Over time these assets will depreciate to zero.

Behavioural finance: The study of the effects of psychology on investors and financial markets.

Cognitive biases: Biases in our thinking that cause us to make decisions based on established norms that may or may not be correct.

Compound interest: Interest calculated on the principal amount invested plus the accumulated interest.

Confirmation bias: The act of interpreting information in a way that is consistent with one's existing beliefs.

Cryptocurrencies: Digital or virtual currencies secured by cryptography, which makes them near impossible to counterfeit or double-spend.

Cultural finance: The combination of cultural theory with conventional finance theory to provide explanations for the behaviours different cultures exhibit with money.

Defensive assets: Assets that are generally designed to provide a steady and/or stable income.

Discretionary spending: A cost that an individual or company can survive without. Non-essential spending.

Dividend: A sum of money paid by a company to its shareholders out of its profits.

Dollar cost averaging (DCA): A strategy in which investment purchases are made at regular intervals regardless of price in an effort to reduce the impact of volatility.

Emotional biases: Spontaneous biases based on our feelings at the time of the decision being made.

Exchange traded funds (ETFs): A basket of securities that tracks and/or mimics an underlying index, sector or asset class.

Fixed interest: An asset class that pays investors a fixed interest payment until its maturity date. At maturity, investors are repaid the principal of the asset. Government and corporate bonds are the most common types of fixed interest.

Fully valued: An investment that, under fundamental analysis, is priced at its true and fair price.

Growth assets: Assets that aim to achieve capital growth.

Hedge fund: A pool of funds managed with a variety of strategies, including buying or selling with borrowed money or securities and trading opaque assets, with the goal of beating standard investment returns.

Heuristic simplification: Decision-making based on simple, fast and 'good-enough' information that allows shortcuts to be made.

Hyperbolic discounting: Valuing immediate though smaller rewards more than long-term larger rewards overall.

Liability: An obligation to pay an economic benefit over time, normally by transferring something like money, goods or services.

Loss aversion: Where a real or potential loss is seen as emotionally more painful than an equivalent or even greater gain.

Meme stock: A listed company that has gained a cult-like following online and through social media platforms.

Perceived value: The perception of a product or service's desirability, especially in comparison to other products or services.

Recency bias: Seeing positive or negative recent events as the most likely long-term outcome.

Round number effect: The disproportionate level of interest in hitting a round number.

S&P 500: The stock market index that tracks the 500 largest listed companies in the US.

S&P/ASX 200: The stock market index that tracks the largest 200 listed companies in Australia.

Self-attribution bias: Attributing successes to personal skills and failures to factors beyond our control.

Shorting or short selling: The act of borrowing a security or securities from a third party for a fee and selling these borrowed holdings in the market. As the market falls the security is brought back at the lower price, making a profit for the short seller. The security is then returned to the third party.

Simple interest: Interest calculated on the principal amount invested.

Term deposit: Money invested at an agreed interest rate for a fixed period of time, normally 12 months or less.

The Reserve Bank of Australia: Australia's central bank. Its duty is to ensure the stability of the Australian dollar, the full employment of the Australian people and Australia's economic prosperity.

Time in the market: Having investments invested in listed markets at every point in a market cycle.

Total returns: The actual rate of return of an investment including interest, capital gains, dividends and distributions coupled with capital appreciation.

About the author

Evan Lucas is an experienced market strategist and a natural communicator and educator. He has loved markets since his days of sitting with his grandfather and mulling over his investment portfolios. What he learned from his early experiences is that investing habits, strategies and behaviours do not necessarily translate across families, generations or peers. This led him to become fascinated with behavioural finance throughout his career, which has taken him to the Netherlands, the UK and back to Australia over a decade and a half. His biggest learning from his time working in markets, investing and finance is that our individual behaviour towards money is always different and always changing.

Evan is a regular media commentator for ABC television and radio news, *The Project*, *SBS World News*, the *Today* show, *Sky News*, *Channel News Asia*, Bloomberg and more.

Acknowledgements

This book would never have come into being without the help of and interactions with countless people – too many to list. To all the people who have helped, shaped, challenged and sharpened me, I can't thank you enough.

There are a few people who I do need to mention because they have been especially helpful.

Julia – Thank you for everything, and for supporting even my most out-there ideas.

Ben – Thank you for making me do this.

Julie, Ian and Audrey – Thank you for everything you gave me.

Nicola – For the foundations.

Lesley – For taking a punt on me.

Brooke – For fixing my 'isms'.

Without your help, feedback and support, *Mind over Money* would not be.

So, thank you.

Index

401(k) 22

ABN Amro 13
American Psychology Association 42
Amsterdam 13
anchoring 26-28
Apple 95, 145
Asian financial crisis 104
Australian Bureau of Statistics 54, 115
Australian Competition and Consumer Commission 148
Australian Institute of Health and Welfare 29
Australian Securities Exchange (ASX) 21
autonomy 55, 64
average earnings 115

bankruptcy 40
banks 125
Barnum, PT 153
bears 24-25
Beichelt, Timm 5

bias 5, 18
bias—attention 31-32
bias—availability 29-31
bias—confirmation 33-34
bias—familiarity 110-111
bias—recency 29, 150
bias—short-term 145
Bitcoin 147
Bryan, William Jennings 55
Bryson, Bill 1
bucket strategy, the 60-64
budgeting 122-125
Buffett, Warren 58, 72-73, 155
bulls 24
buy now pay later 33, 42, 68

Cambridge University 36
Campbell, Angus 55
Camus, Albert 35
car insurance 126-127
cash 81, 148
casinos 30
Chanel, Coco 46
China 80-81

choice 4, 55-64
Clear, James 23
climate change 126
collectivism 84, 85
communication 49-51
competition 15
compound interest 69-73
control 55-57, 121-131
corrections 103-104
COVID-19 92, 101-102, 104, 132-134, 150
credit cards 128
crisis management 116-117
cryptocurrency 30-31, 147-148
cultural differences 78-79, 82-84
culture 80-94

debt 77-78
debt—bad 39-40, 41-42, 117
debt—good 40
debtor, the 41-42
decision-making 2-3
discounting 66-68
diversification 105-111
divorce 48
dollar cost averaging 138-140, 158
dopamine 134-135, 137-138

echo chambers 33
economists 4
Einstein, Albert 71
El Capitan 98
elephant paradigm, the 113
emotions 5
energy bills 128-129
equities 148-149

European Central Bank 81
Evensky, Harold 60
expectations 143-151

fear 97-98, 105
fear of missing out (FOMO) 40, 108-109, 136
Federal Reserve Bank Philadelphia 40
femininity 83
financial infidelity 53
first impressions 26-27
fixed costs 123-124, 130
Fresco, Jacque 143

gambling 29-30, 145
GameStop 31-32
Germany 81
get-even-itis 87-88
Global Financial Crisis 14, 74-76, 104
goals 117, 137-138, 141-142
gold 81
golden rectangle 95-97
greater fool theory 147

habits 135
health insurance 127-128
Hens, Dr Thorsten 84, 87
Herrnstein, Richard 67
heuristics 25-34
Hofstede, Geert 81-83
home insurance 126-127
home loans 77, 125-126
Homo economicus 4-5
Homo emotionalis 5

Honnold, Alex 98, 106
household wealth 115, 118-119
hyperbolic discounting 67-68, 145

ignorer, 43-44
impulse buys 136
India 81
individualism 84, 85
indulgence 83
insurance 126-128
investor, the 43

Jobs Steve 95
Journal of Consumer Psychology 40
Journal of Personality and Social Psychology 55, 64

Kahneman, Daniel 20, 32, 87
Keats, John 95

Laibson, David 68
lazy tax 129
Locke, John 10-11
loss aversion 19-23, 84-86
lottery 29-30, 40, 121, 145

Markowitz, Harry 106-108, 110
masculinity 83, 85
ME Bank 133
Mediterranean cultures 85
meme stocks 30-31
Mexican fisherman story 59-60
Mill, John Stuart 4
modern portfolio theory 106-108
money identity 9-15
money personalities 35-45
mortgages 125-126
MSCI 149

Natixis 146
Nobel Prize 5, 106

orientation 83
overconfidence 23-24

PayPal 136
Peck, M Scott 17
perspective 113-120
piggy bank 37
pocket money 37
power bills 128-129
power distance 83, 85, 86-88
property—commercial 148
property—residential 24-25

reasonableness 7
Reddit 31
relationships 35-36, 46-54
Relationships Australia 54
Reserve Bank of Australia 125
restraint 83
retail therapy 134
retirement funds 22, 61, 63, 157
returns—delayed 3, 66-68, 145
returns—immediate 2, 66-67
returns—realistic 148-150
Rieger, Dr Marc Oliver 84, 87
ringfencing 109-110
risk 20-21, 38, 87-88, 106-107, 144, 148-151
Rushdie, Salman 113

saver, the 38-39
savings 28, 80-81
Schroders 145-146
self-attribution 23-25

Seuss, Dr. 121
shame 50-51
shared finances 46-54, 154
shares 139-140, 149
shopper's high 40
shorting 31-32
Siegel, Jeremy 95
Simon, Herbert A 5, 7
social media 33, 115
speculation 146-148
spender, the 39-41
spending 49
spendvesting 132-142
Stokvels 86
Stone Age 1
strengths 53-54
superannuation 22, 61, 63, 157

Tanda 85-86
time 58-60, 65-79
Tolstoy, Leo 65
Tversky, Amos 20, 87

uncertainty avoidance 83, 88-89
University of Michigan 36
US National Safety Council 30

Wang, Dr Mei 84, 87
waste 136
Watts, Alan 4
Weimar Republic 81
Westpac 133
Wilde, Oscar 9

Yosemite National Park 98

zero-interest schemes 42, 68